Classical Guitar Tunes

O'Carolan Airs

by Guido Böger

The Corona model Madagascar Rosewood with Cedar Top/Cutaway guitar image on the cover is courtesy of Prenkert Guitars.

WWW.MELBAY.COM

Foreword

In this, my third volume of the works of Turlough O'Carolan (1670-1738), I strive once more to achieve a 'baroquesque' style in these arrangements, complete with clear harmonizations. I have also sought a balance between interpreting the melodies themselves and the integration of secondary musical lines, giving a special eye towards the ease of execution, as well as an optimal sound throughout.

Along with their companions, found in my first two volumes, the Airs of O'Carolan are now completely set with this edition. Last but not least, I would like to thank my wife, Margaret Ellen Fitzgerald, once again for her help, support and musical feedback in preparing this manuscript.

Guido Böger

Remarks:

1. The tempo and character markings at the beginning of the pieces reflect those used in the standard printed editions of these works.

2. "Catherine Martin" is arranged here twice, once in the more usual Dorian mode, and also in a less commonly interpreted Mixolydian alternative.

3. Appogiaturas: The grace notes should generally be played before the beat, as short anticipatory figures.

   a) without a rest, they are attached to the note of the upper/lower voice, respectively

   b) with a rest, they are separated from the note of the upper/lower voice

Contents

Title	Page
Dr. John Hart, Bishop of Achonry	4
Mrs. Costello	6
Sir Ulick Burke	7
Thomas Burke	8
Betty O'Brien	10
Mrs. O'Connor	11
Maurice O'Connor, First Air	12
Maurice O'Connor, Third Air	14
Michael O'Connor, First Air	16
Michael O'Connor, Second Air	18
Nancy Copper, Second Air	19
Denis O'Connor, First Air	20
Bridget Cruise, First Air	22
Bridget Cruise, Second Air	23
Bridget Cruise, Third Air	24
Bridget Cruise, Fourth Air	25
John Drury, First Air	26
John Drury, Second Air	27
Lord Dillon	28
Fanny Dillon	30
Counsellor Dillon	31
Mrs. Edwards	32
Mrs. Fallon	33
Mrs. Farrell	34
Mrs. Garvey, First Air	36
Kean O'Hara, First Air	37
Kean O'Hara, Second Air	38
Kean O'Hara, Third Air	40
John O'Reilly, Second Air	42
Patrick Kelly	44
Planxty Kelly	45
Mrs. Judge	46
Thomas Judge, or Carolan's Frolic	48
Lord Louth	49
Mrs. MacDermott Roe	50
Mrs. Anne MacDermott Roe	51
Elizabeth MacDermott Roe	52
Edmond MacDermott Roe	53
John MacDermott	54
Miss Fetherston, or Carolan's Devotion	57
Betty MacNeill	58
Captain Magan	59
Kitty Magennis	60
Mrs. Maxwell, Second Air	62
Planxty O'Rourke, First Air	63
Planxty O'Rourke, Second Air	64
Lord Massereene	66
James Daly	69
Miss Noble	70
Mrs. Nugent	72
Elizabeth Nugent	74
John Nugent	76
Grace Nugent	77
Mr. Waller	78
Mrs. Waller	80
Mrs. Delany	82
Sir Charles Coote	84
Daniel Kelly	86
Catherine Martin (Dorian Mode)	88
Catherine Martin (Mixolydian Mode)	89
Brian Maguire	90
Planxty O'Carolan	91

Dr. John Hart, Bishop of Achonry

Turlough O'Carolan
1670-1738

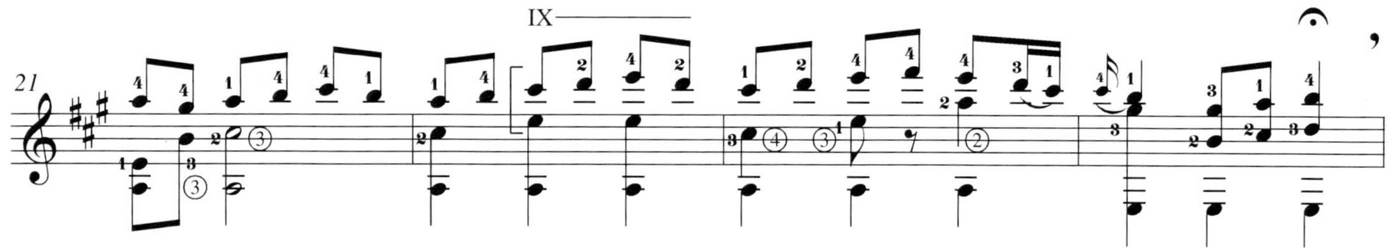

21
IX

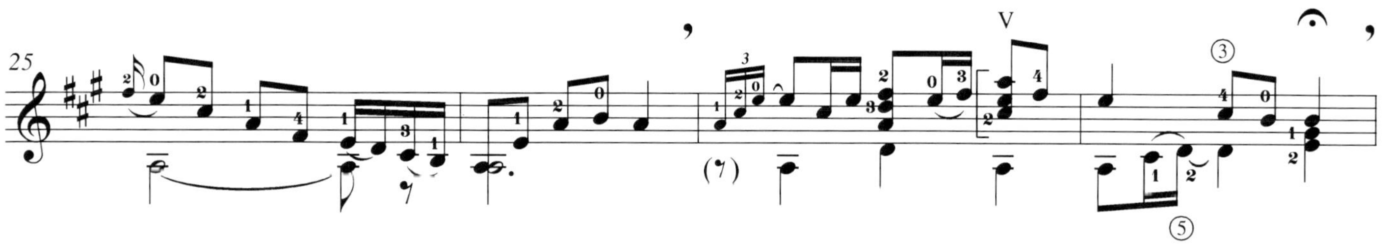

25
V

29

Mrs.Costello

Turlough O'Carolan

Sir Ulick Burke

Turlough O'Carolan

Thomas Burke

Turlough O'Carolan

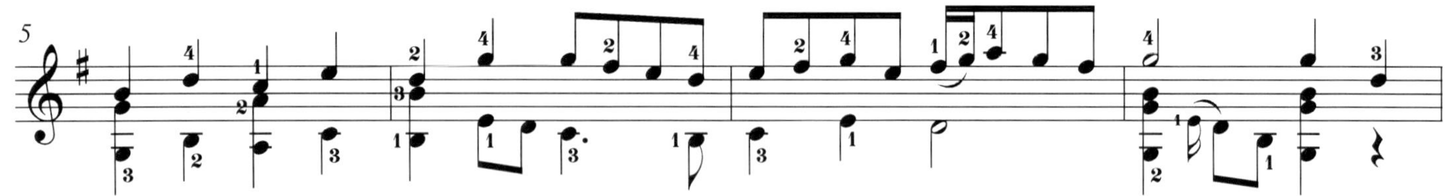

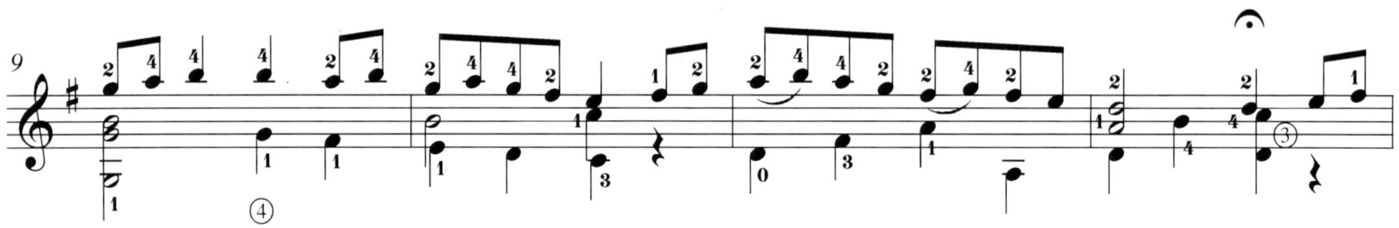

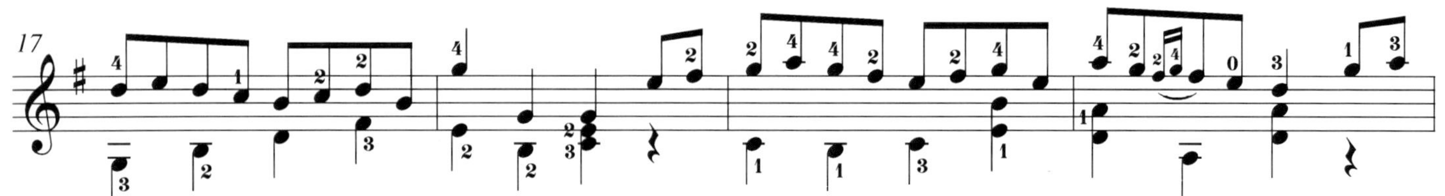

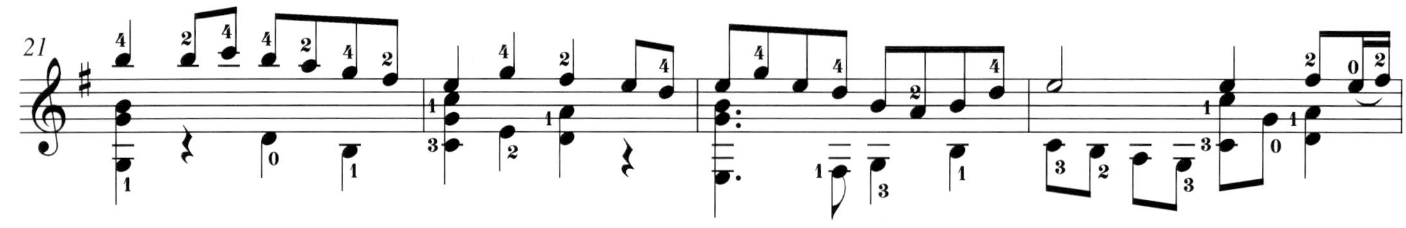

meno mosso, a piacere
III

Betty O'Brien

Turlough O'Carolan

Mrs. O'Connor

Turlough O'Carolan

Moderato

Maurice O'Connor, First Air

Turlough O'Carolan

Maurice O'Connor, Third Air

Turlough O'Carolan

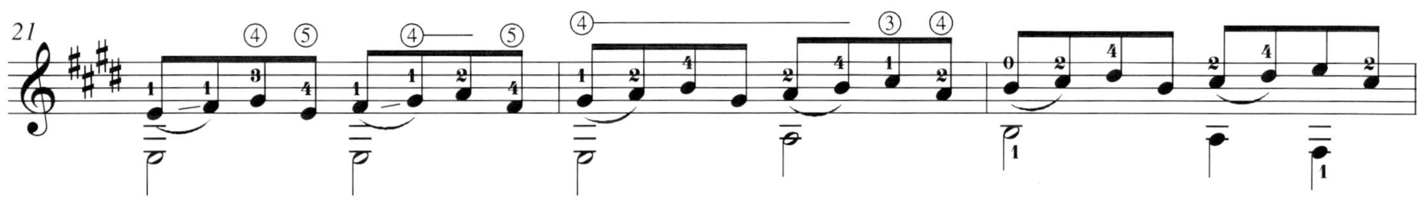

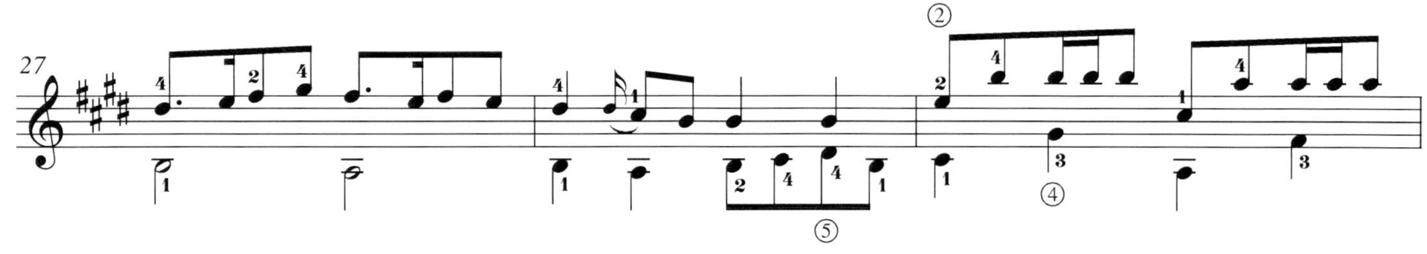

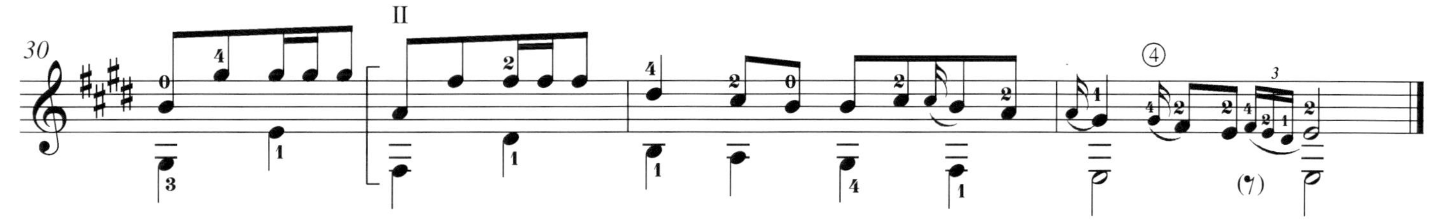

Michael O'Connor, First Air

Turlough O'Carolan

Allegretto

Jig

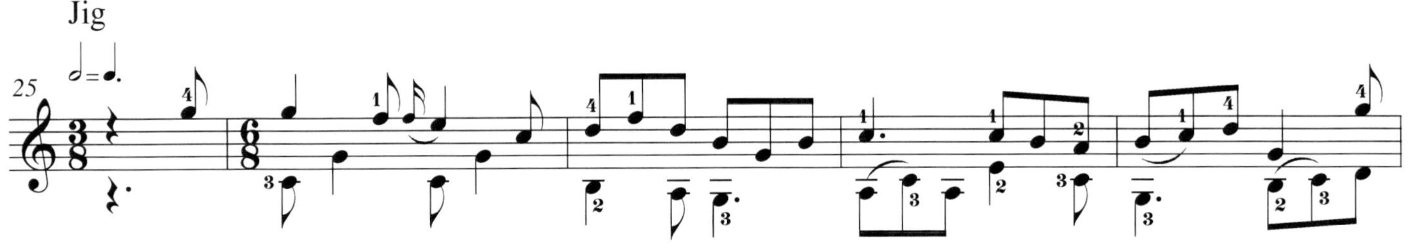

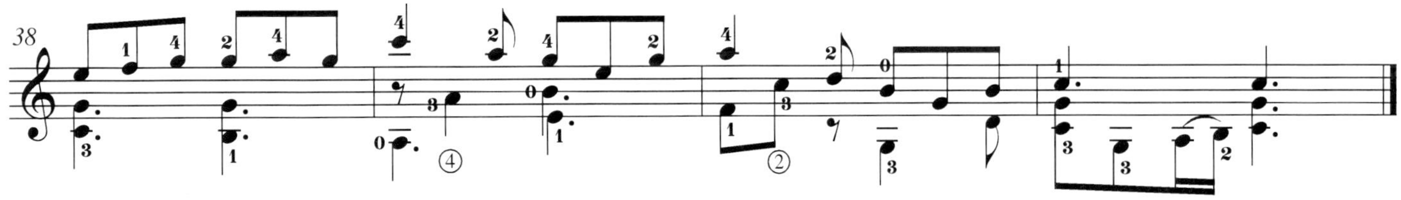

Michael O'Connor, Second Air

Turlough O'Carolan

Nancy Cooper, Second Air

Turlough O'Carolan

Denis O'Connor, First Air

Turlough O'Carolan

Moderato

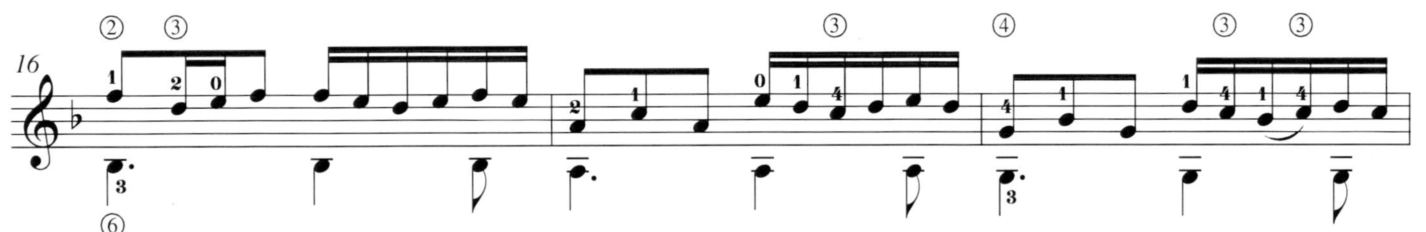

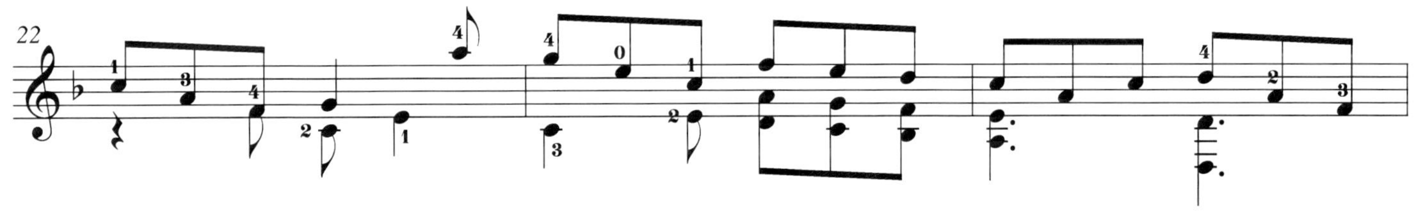
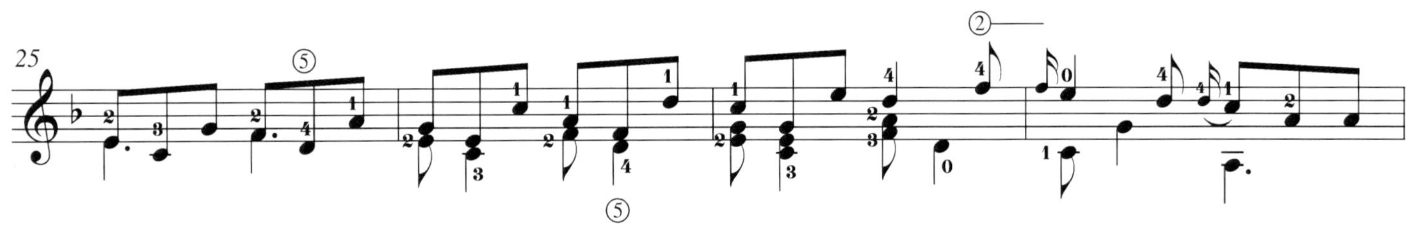
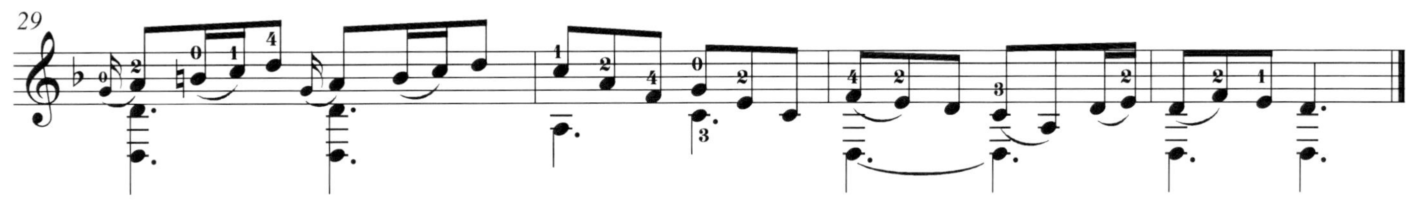

Bridget Cruise, First Air

Turlough O'Carolan

Bridget Cruise, Second Air

Turlough O'Carolan

Bridget Cruise, Third Air

Turlough O'Carolan

Bridget Cruise, Fourth Air

Turlough O'Carolan

John Drury, First Air

Turlough O'Carolan

John Drury, Second Air

Turlough O'Carolan

Lord Dillon

Turlough O'Carolan

Moderato

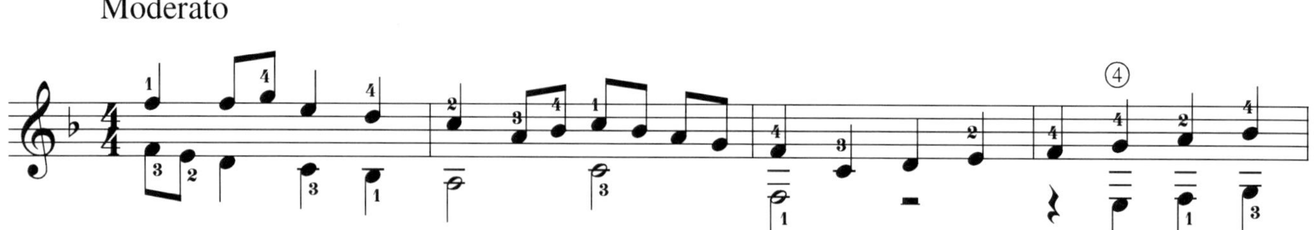

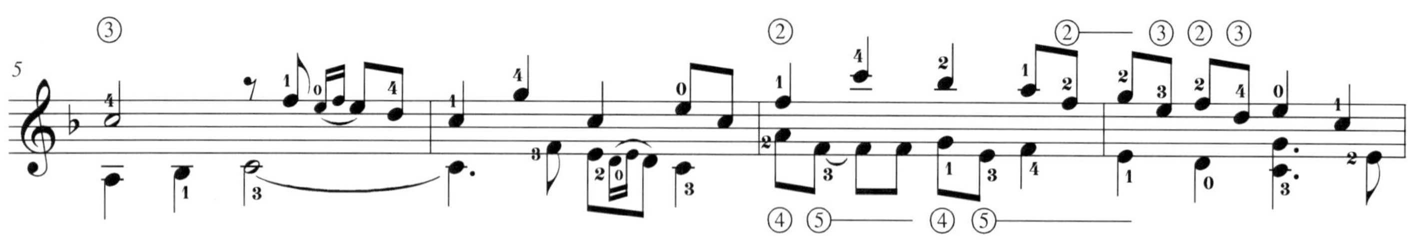

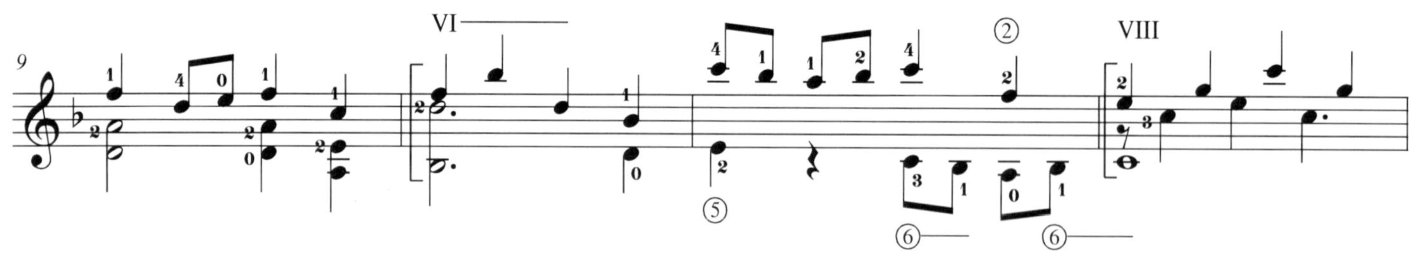

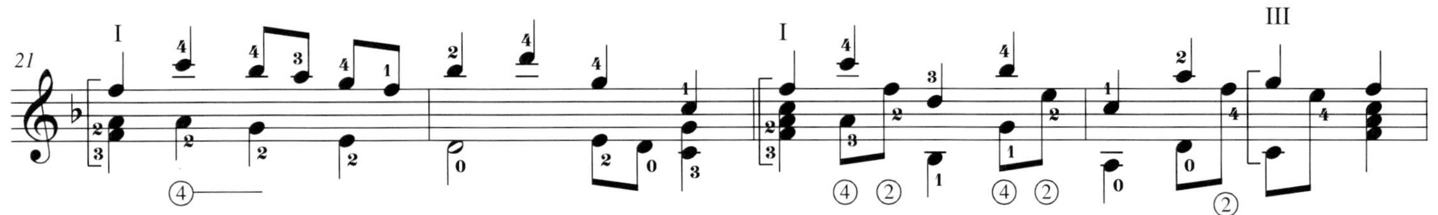
21
I
I
III

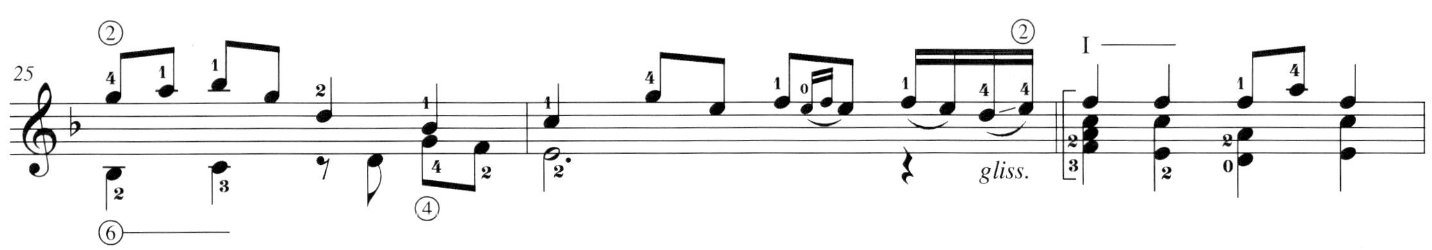
25
gliss.
I

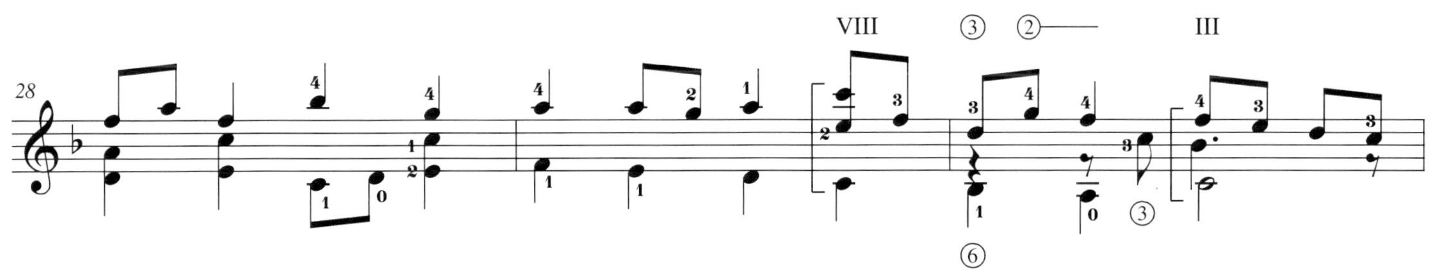
28
VIII
III

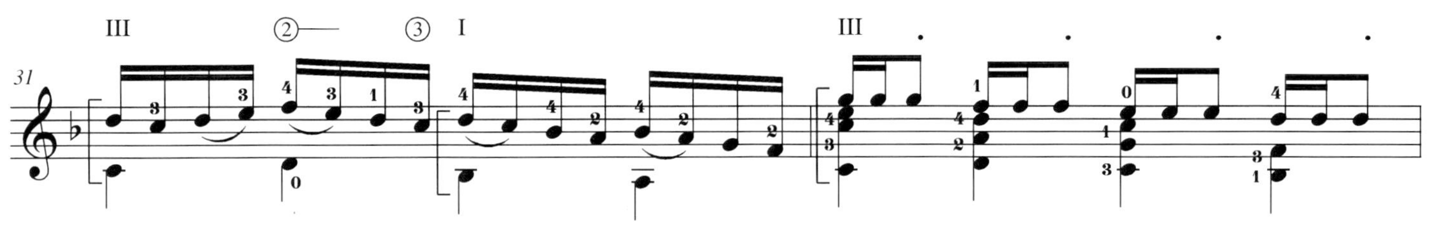
31
III
I
III

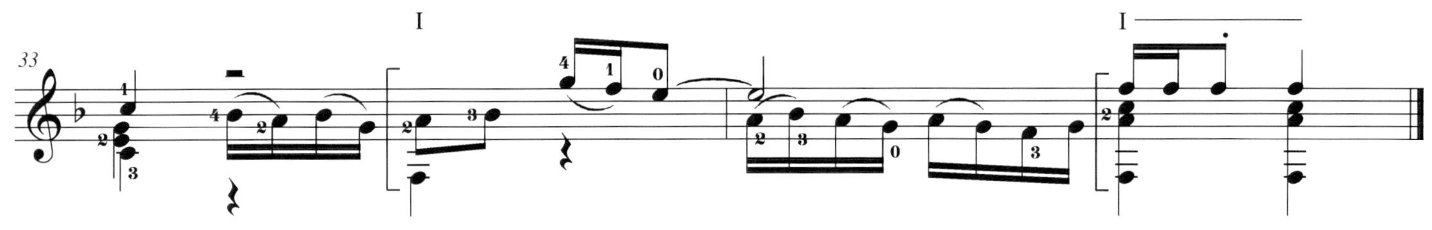
33
I
I

Fanny Dillon

Turlough O'Carolan

Counsellor Dillon

Turlough O'Carolan

Mrs. Edwards

Turlough O'Carolan

Mrs. Fallon

Turlough O'Carolan

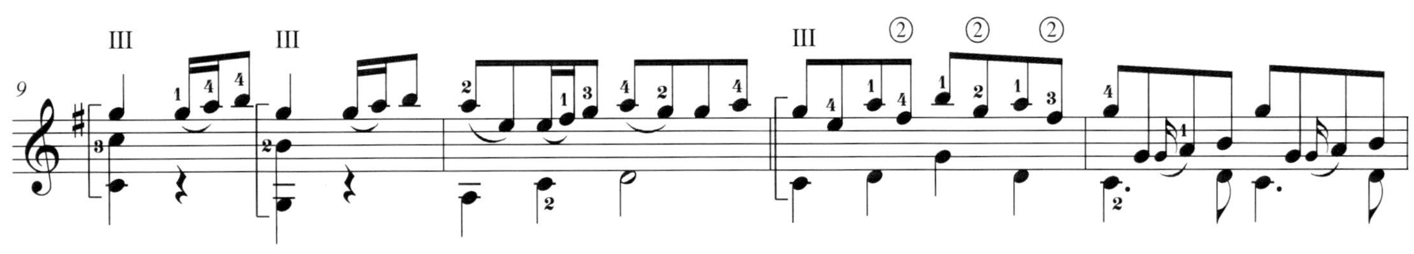

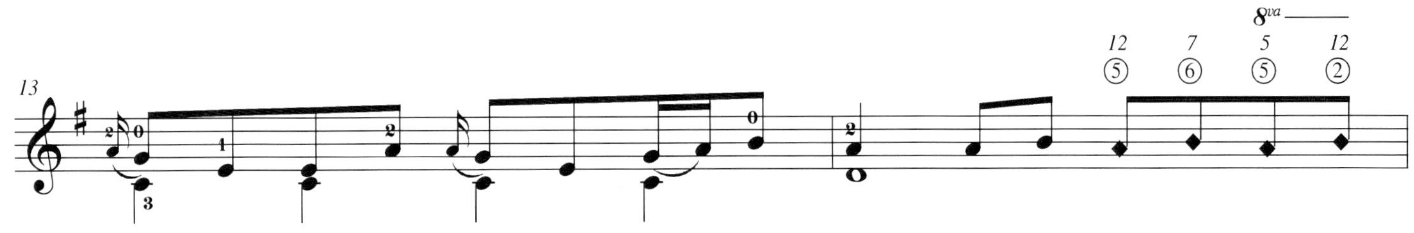

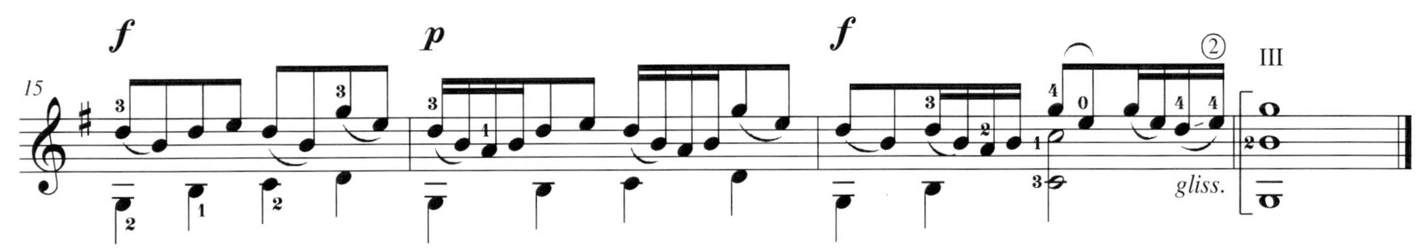

Mrs. Farrell

Turlough O'Carolan

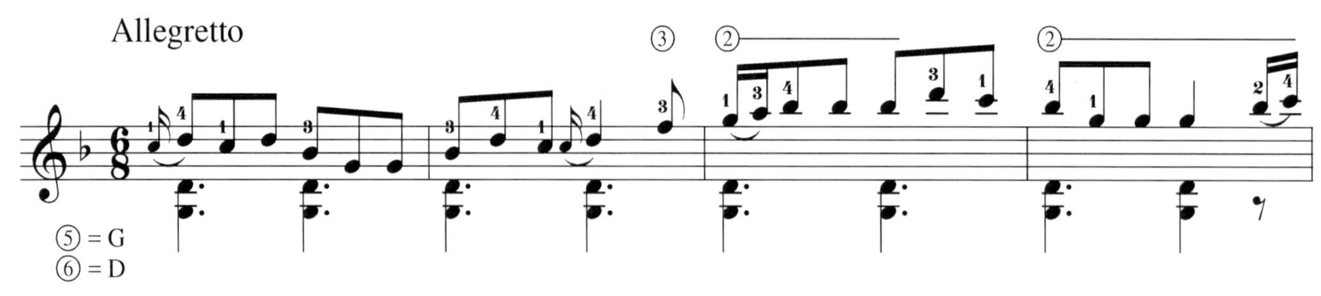

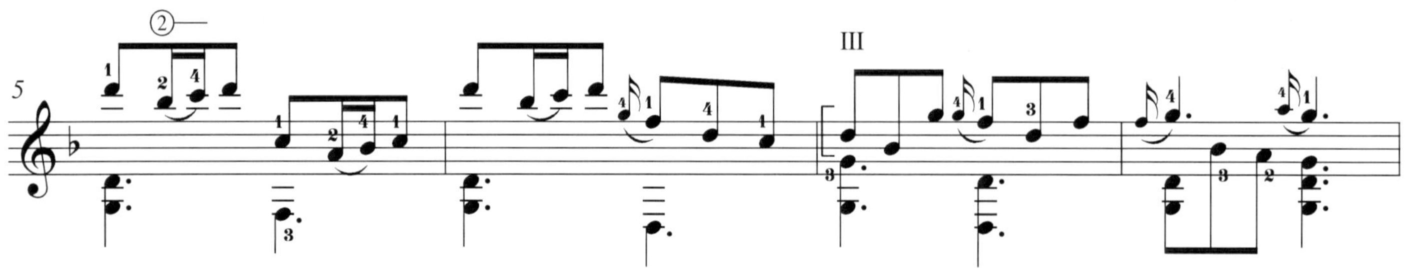

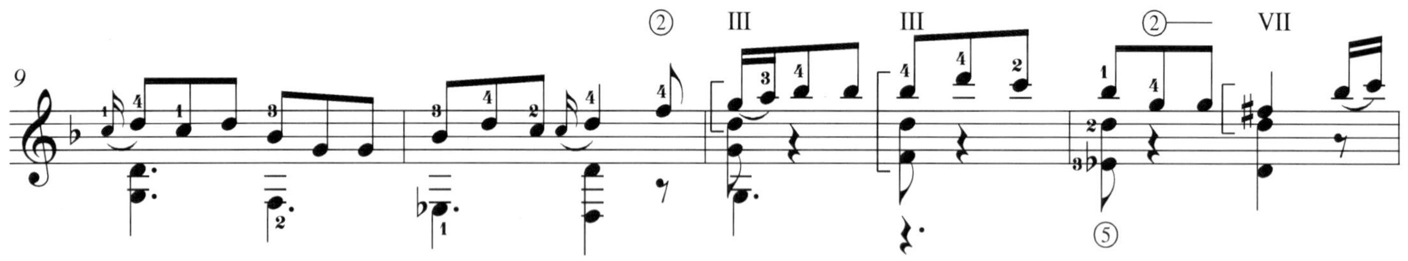

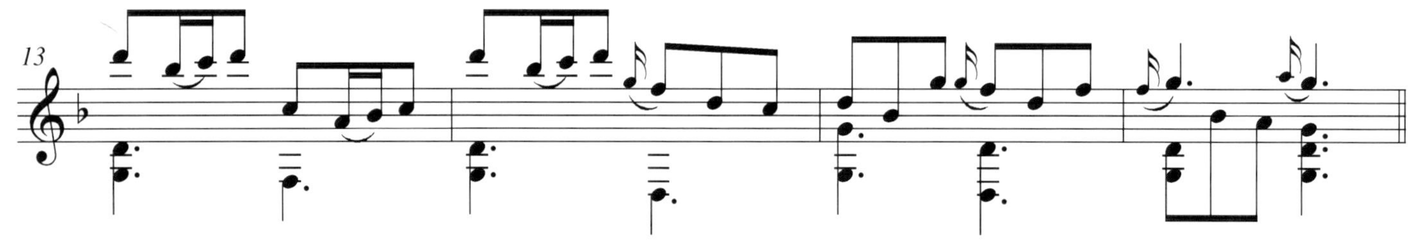

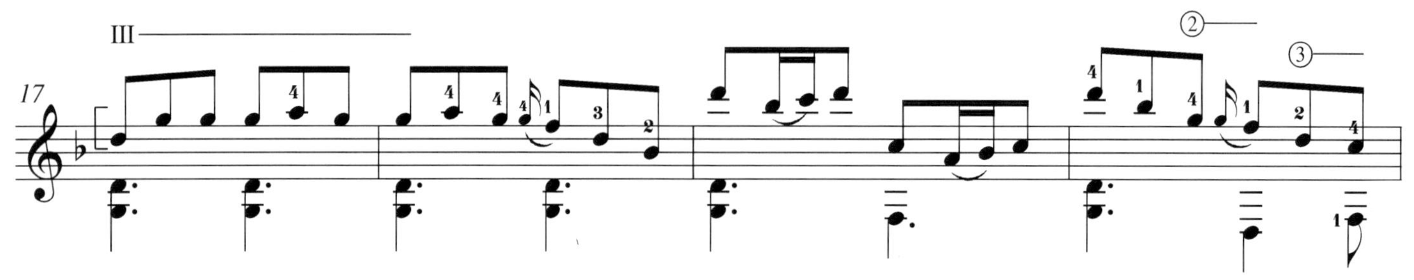

21
③
③
③
gliss.

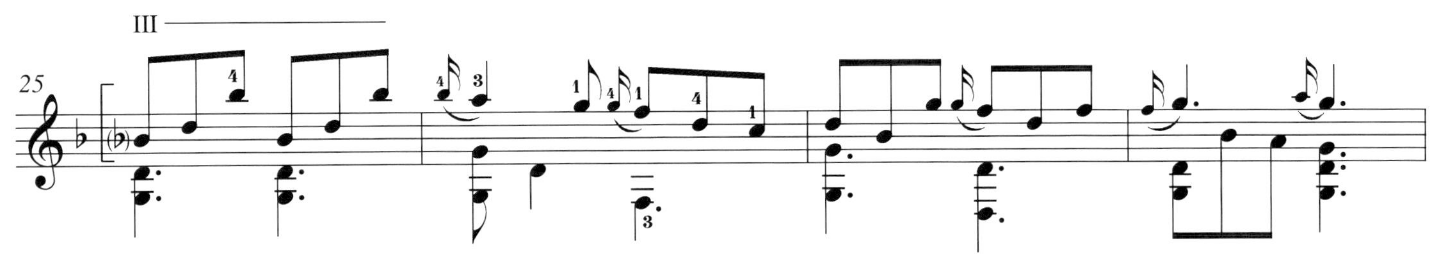
III
25

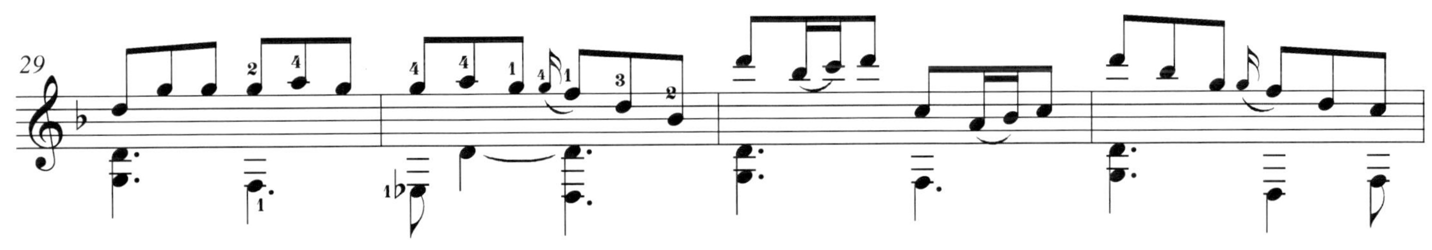
29

33

37
III

Mrs. Garvey, First Air

Turlough O'Carolan

Kean O'Hara, First Air

Turlough O'Carolan

Kean O'Hara, Second Air

Turlough O'Carolan

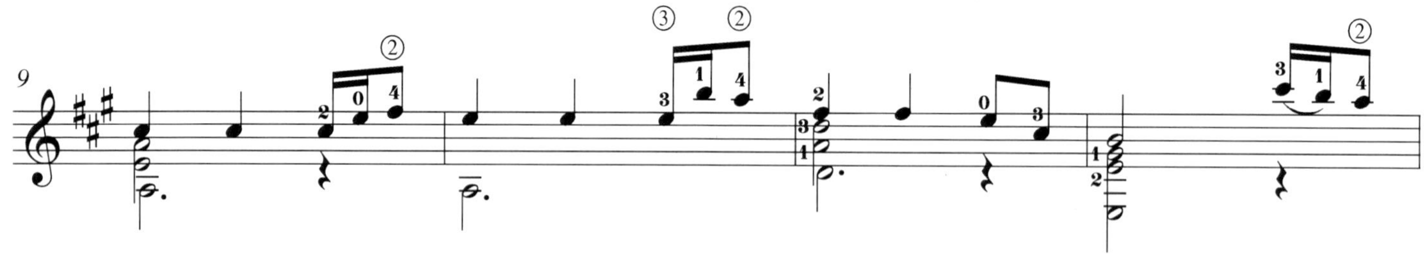

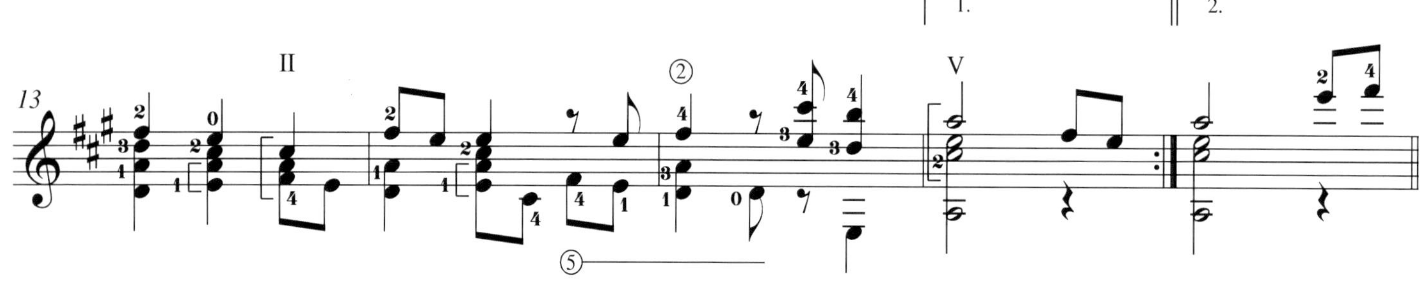

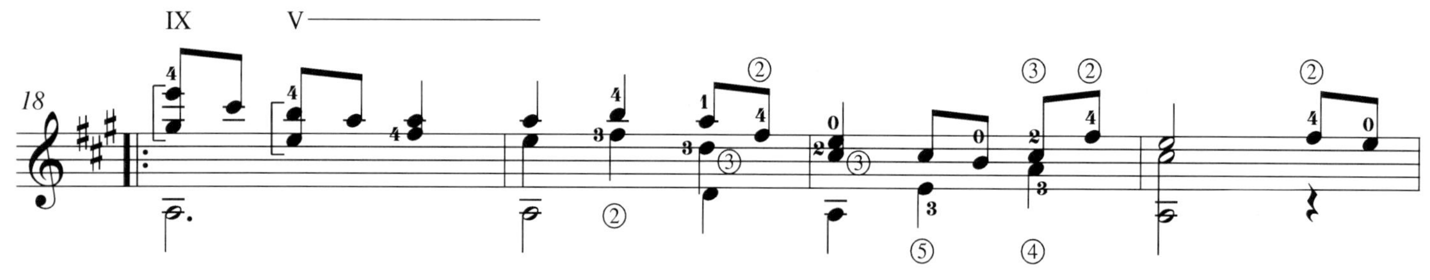

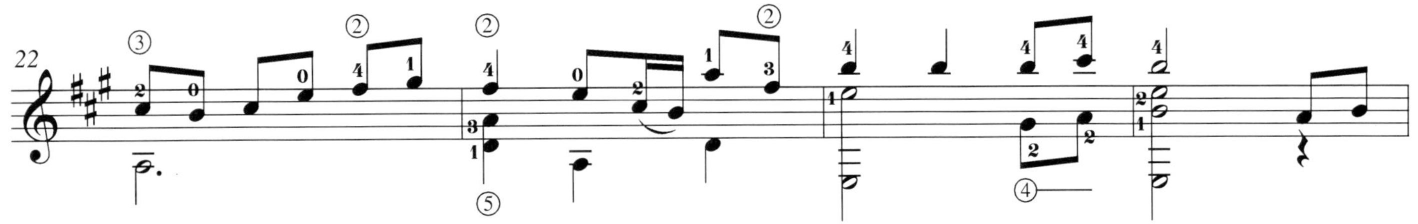
22

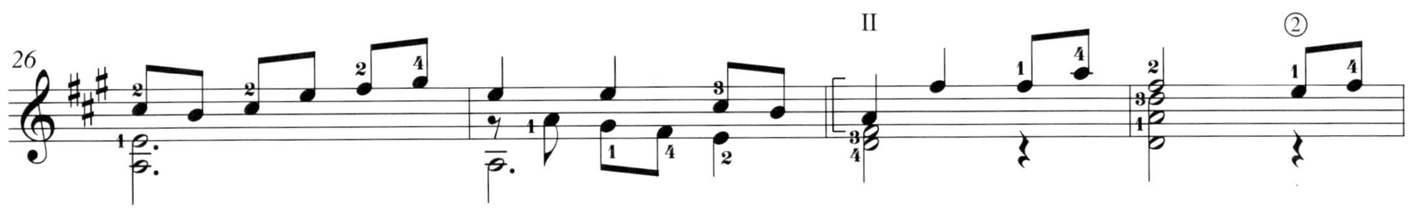
26
II

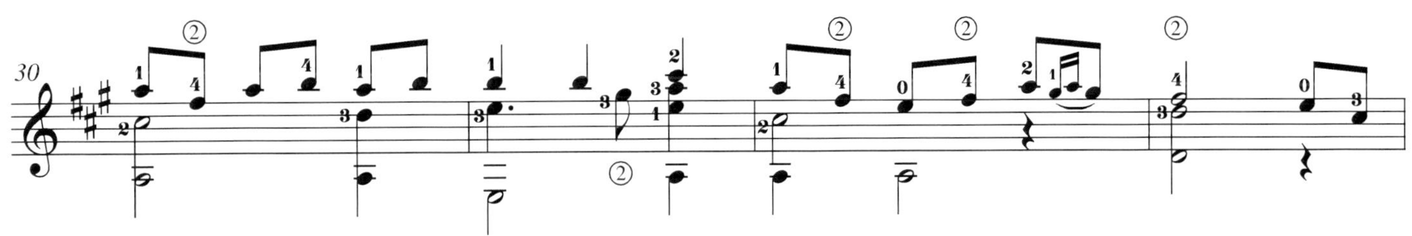
30

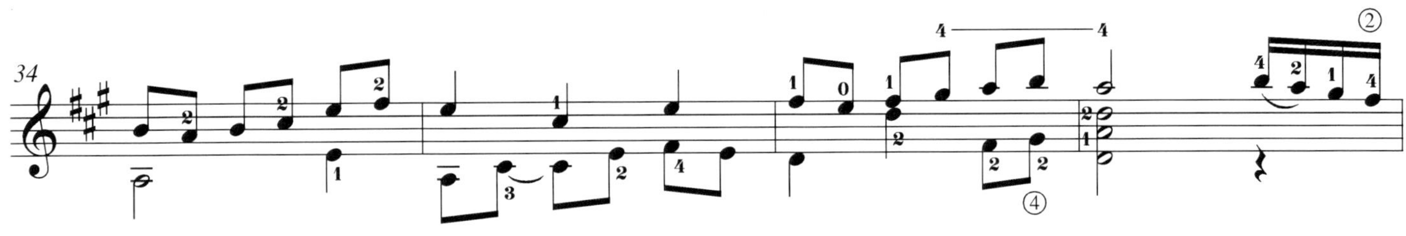
34

38
II
1.
2.

Kean O'Hara, Third Air

Turlough O'Carolan

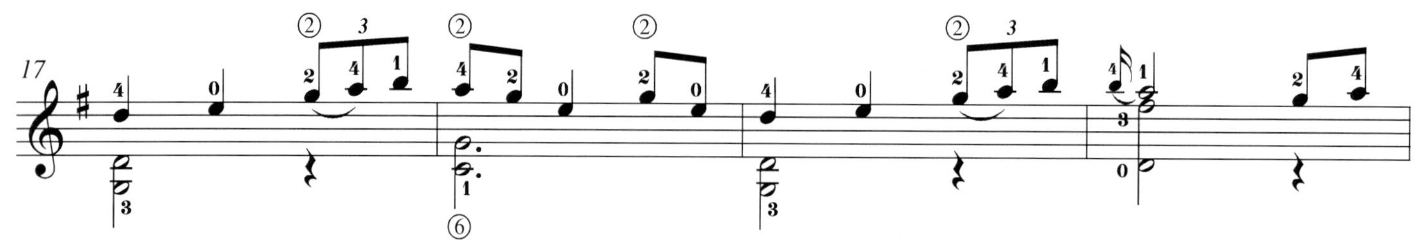

21
3
2
3
1
1

25
3
3
3
4
1

29
1
3
2
2
1
2
4
3

John O'Reilly, Second Air

Turlough O'Carolan

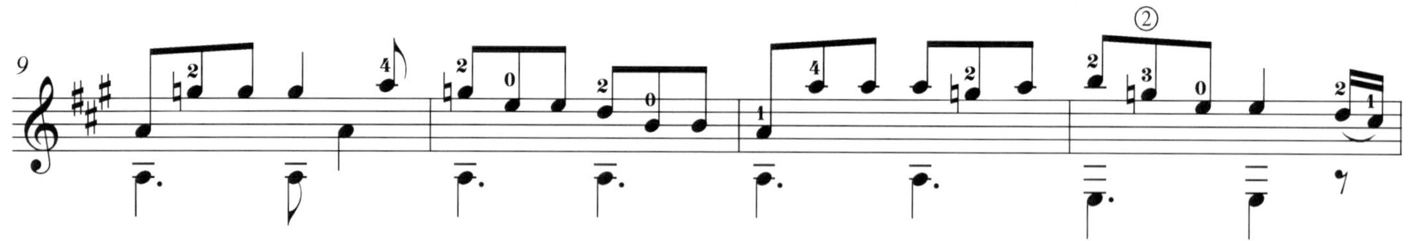

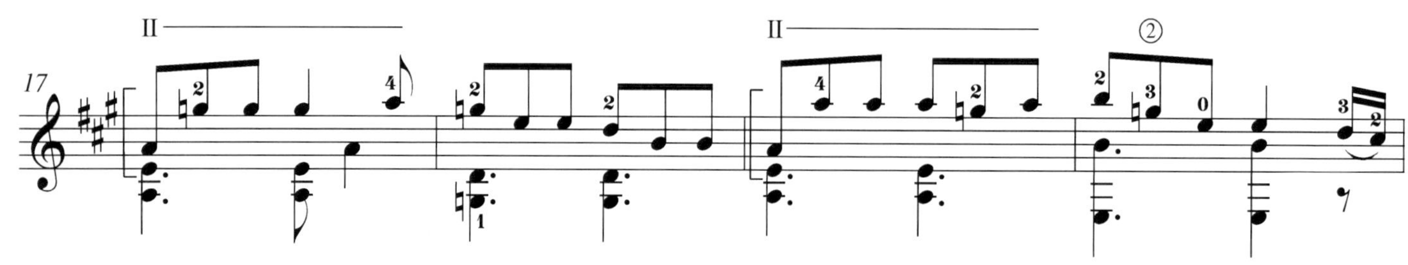

21
II
3
2
4
1
3
1
3
1

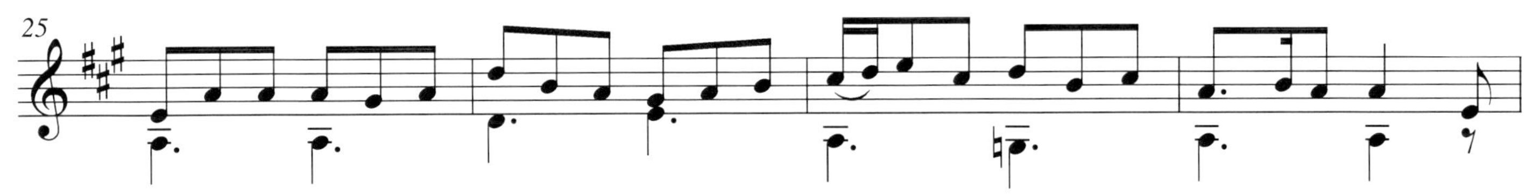
25

29

Patrick Kelly

Turlough O'Carolan

Planxty Kelly

Turlough O'Carolan

Moderato

Mrs. Judge

Turlough O'Carolan

Jig
VII
III
II
1.
2.

Thomas Judge, or Carolan's Frolic

Turlough O'Carolan

Lord Louth

Turlough O'Carolan

Mrs. MacDermott Roe

Mrs. Anne MacDermott Roe

Turlough O'Carolan

Elizabeth MacDermott Roe

Turlough O'Carolan

Andante espressivo

Edmond MacDermott Roe

Turlough O'Carolan

John MacDermott

Turlough O'Carolan

più mosso

29
31
33
a
i m
a i
35
37
rallentando
meno mosso
39
41
rit.
II
8va

Miss Fetherston, or Carolan's Devotion

Turlough O'Carolan

Andante con moto

Betty MacNeill

Turlough O'Carolan

Allegretto

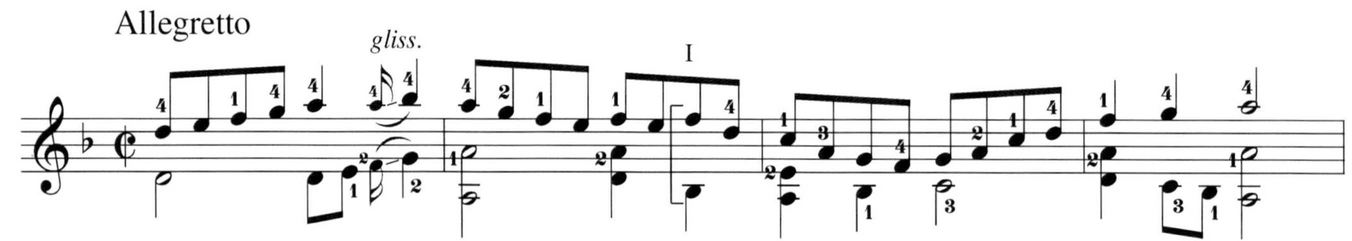

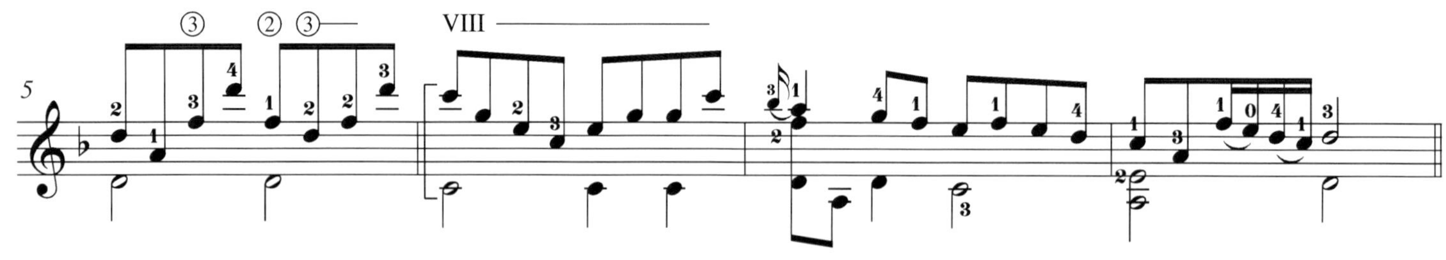

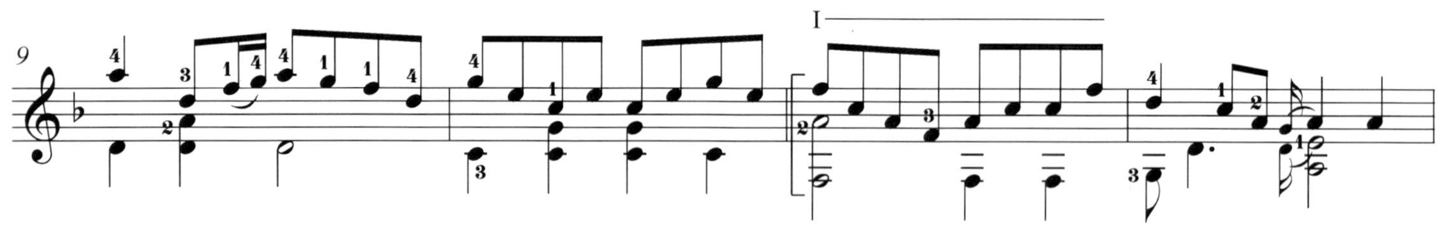

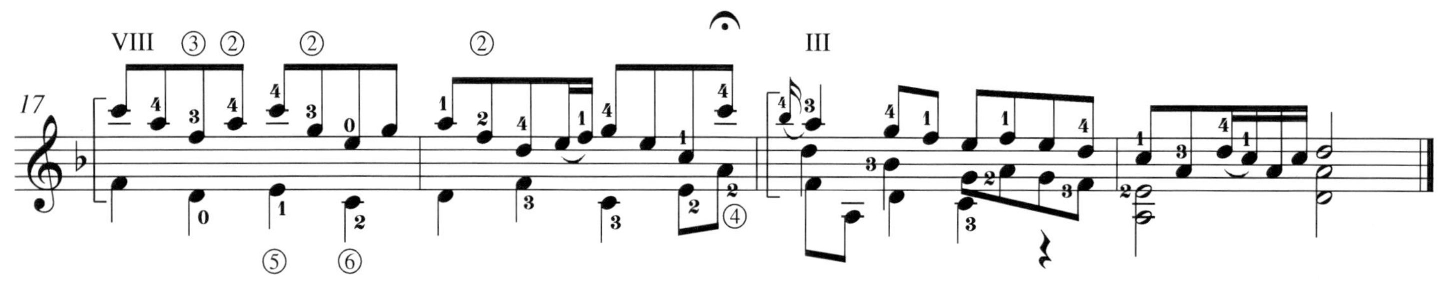

Captain Magan

Turlough O'Carolan

Kitty Magennis

Turlough O'Carolan

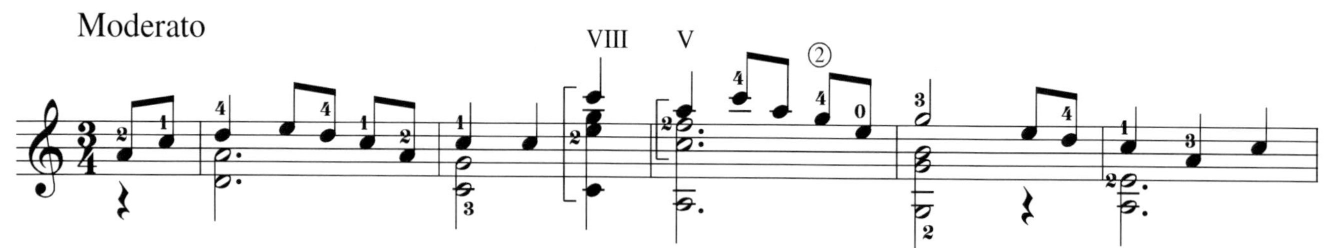

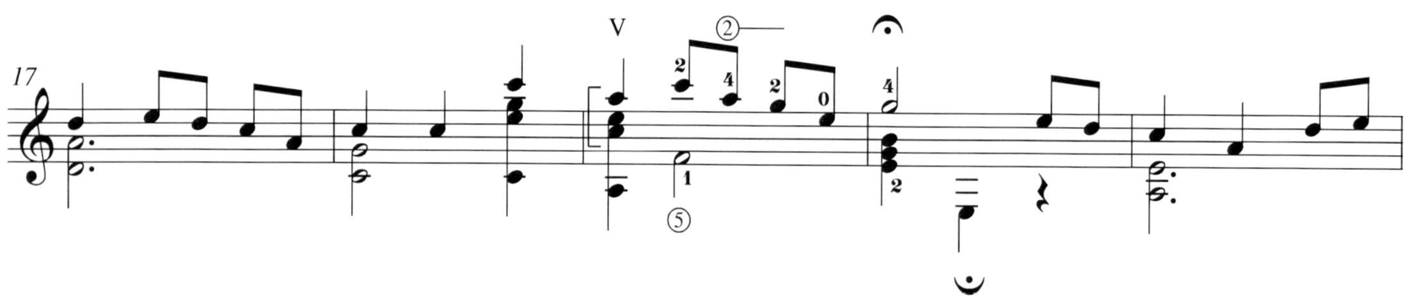

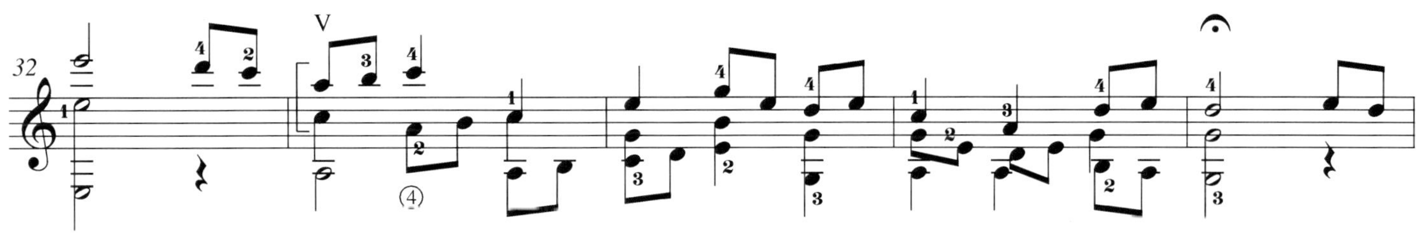

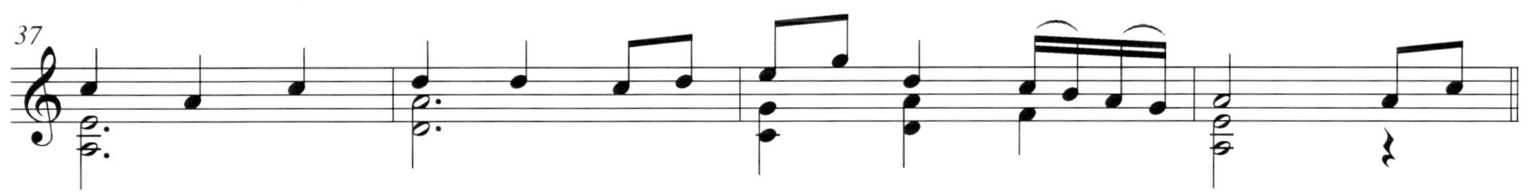

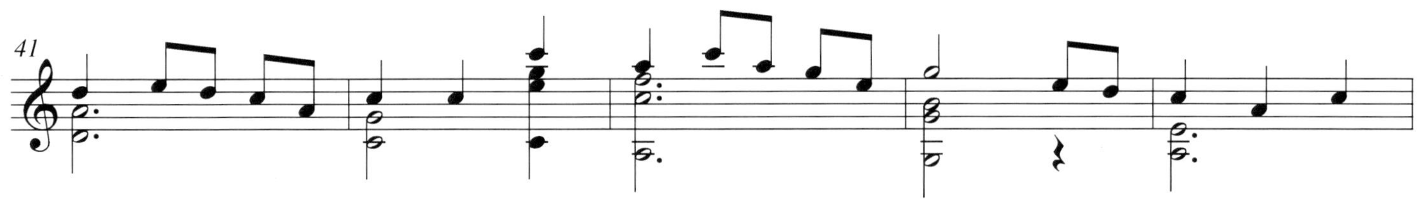

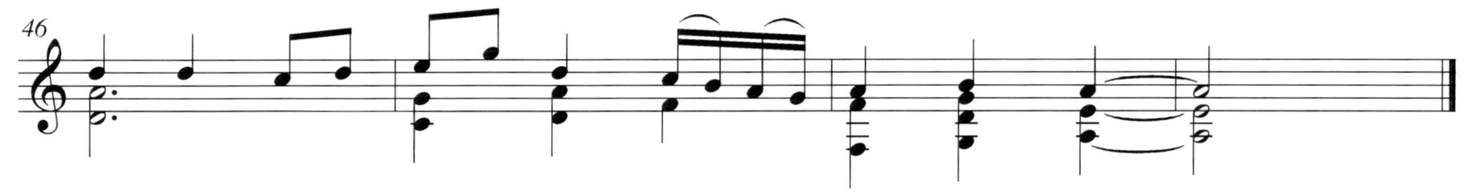

Mrs. Maxwell, Second Air

Turlough O'Carolan

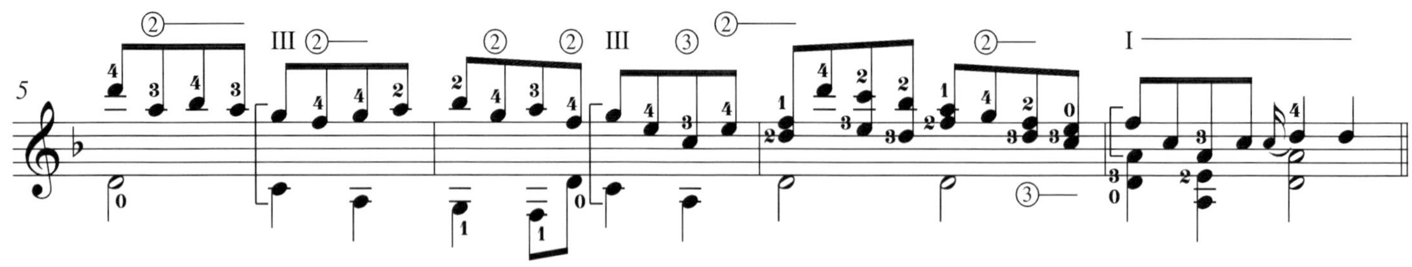

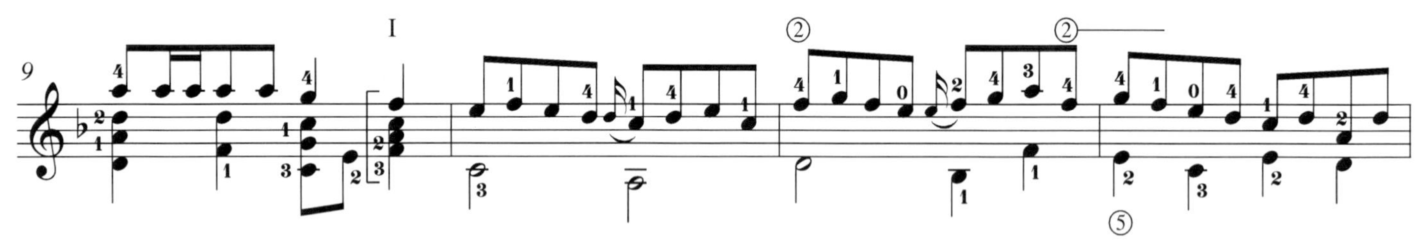

Planxty O'Rourke, First Air

Turlough O'Carolan

Allegro ma non troppo

Planxty O'Rourke, Second Air

Turlough O'Carolan

32

37
gliss.
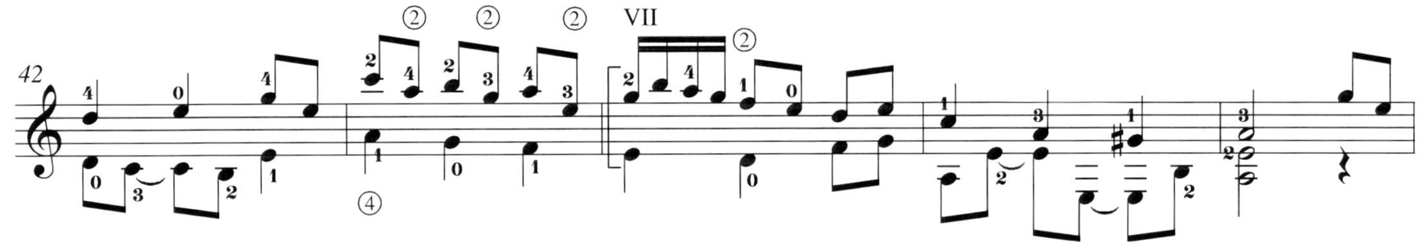
42
VII
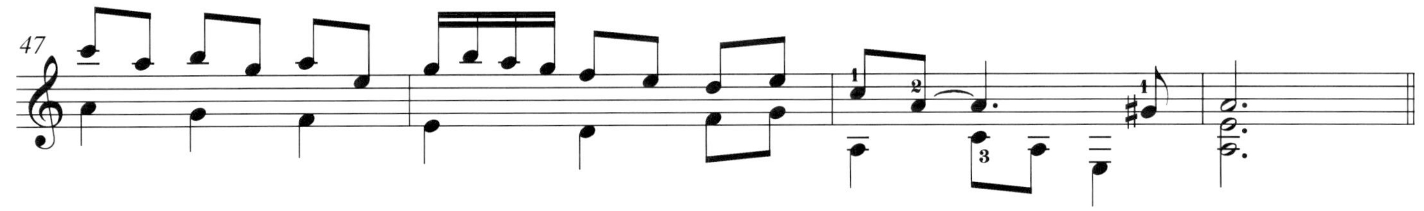
47

51
III
III
III

57

Lord Massereene

Turlough O'Carolan

49
I
gliss.
③
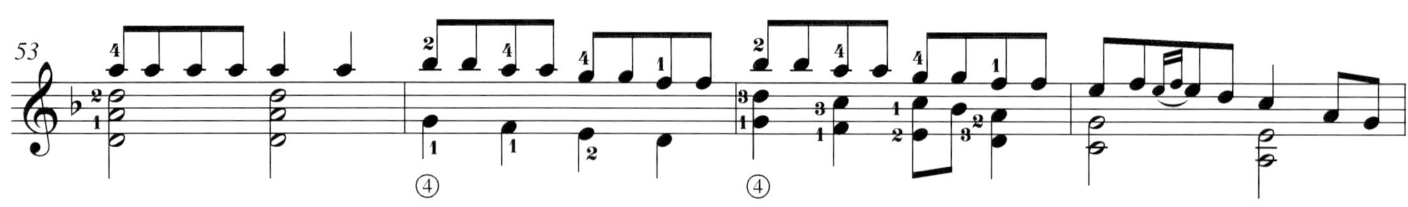
53
④
④

57

61
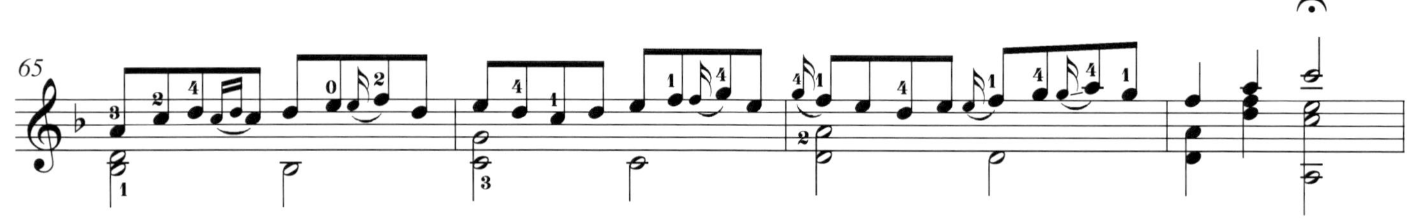
65

69

James Daly

Turlough O'Carolan

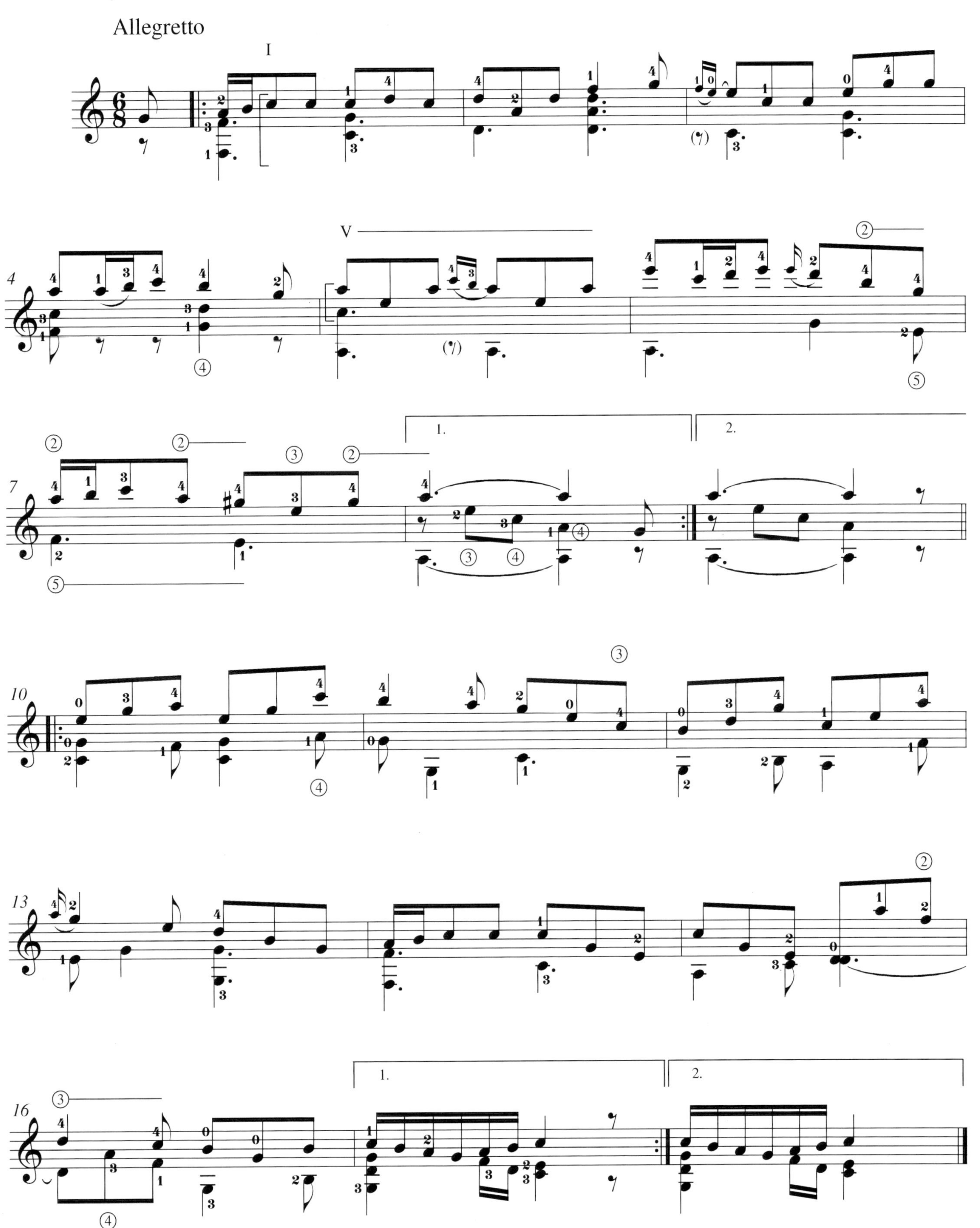

Miss Noble

Turlough O'Carolan

II
gliss.
III

Mrs. Nugent

Turlough O'Carolan

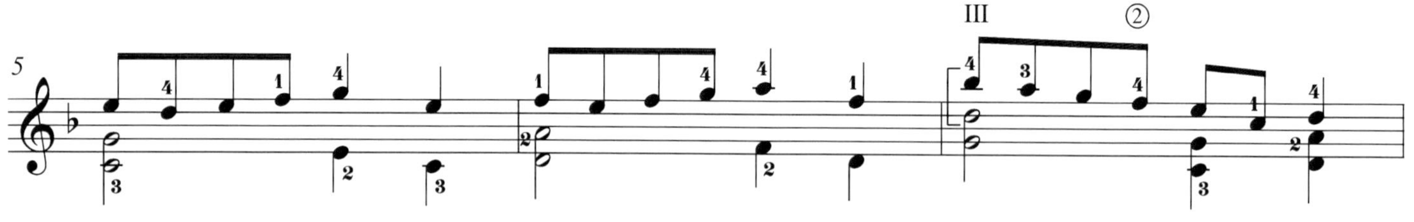

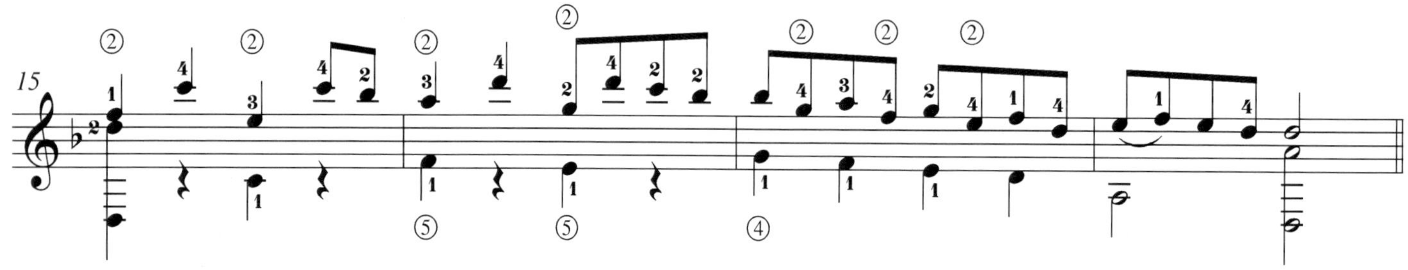

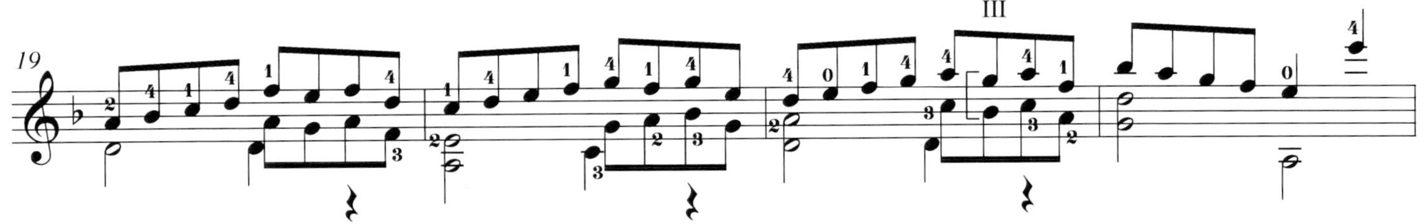
19
III
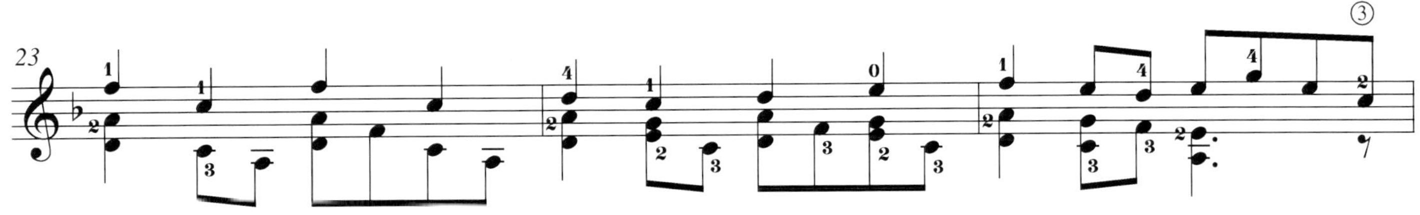
23

26

30

34
V

Elizabeth Nugent

Turlough O'Carolan

Moderato

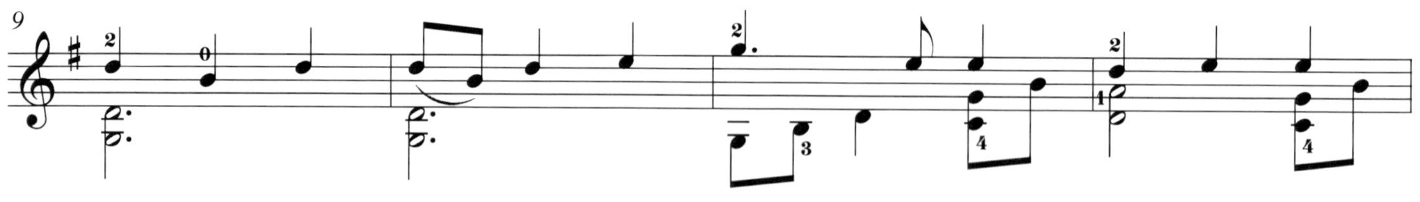

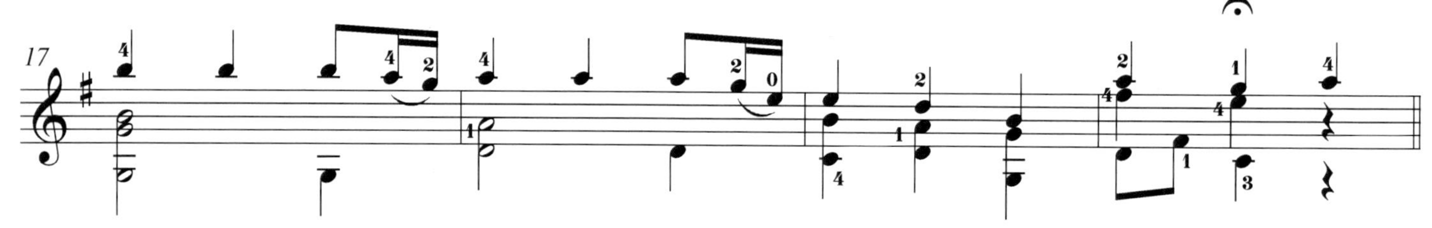

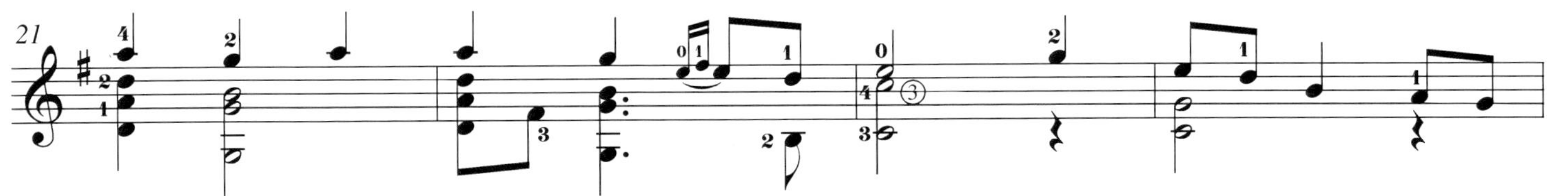
21

25

29

33

37
gliss.

John Nugent

Turlough O'Carolan

Allegretto

Grace Nugent

Turlough O'Carolan

Allegretto

Mr. Waller

Turlough O'Carolan

Andante con moto

Mrs. Waller

Turlough O'Carolan

Allegretto

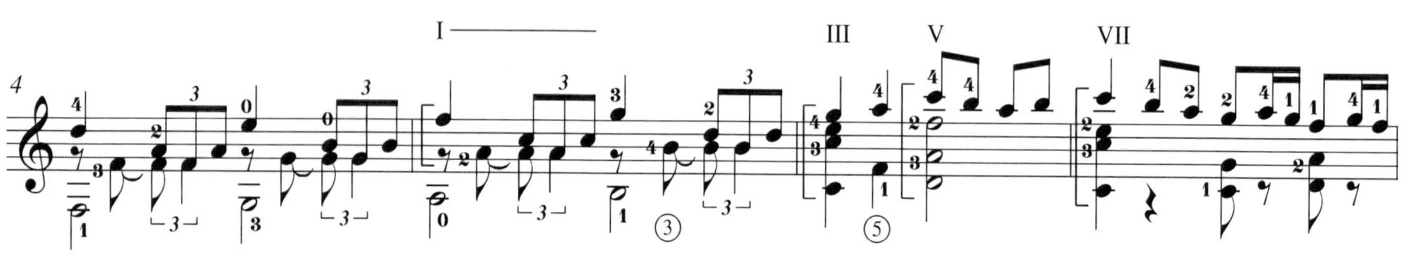

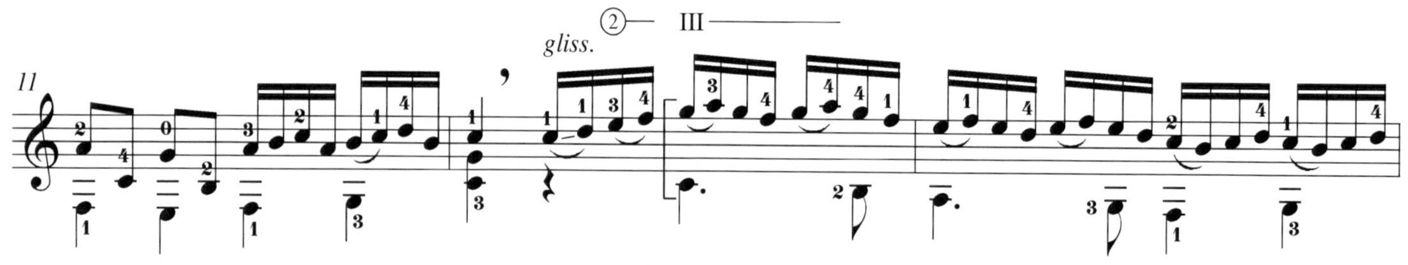

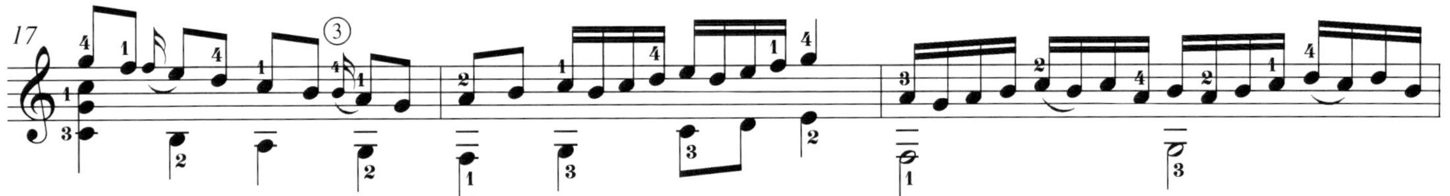

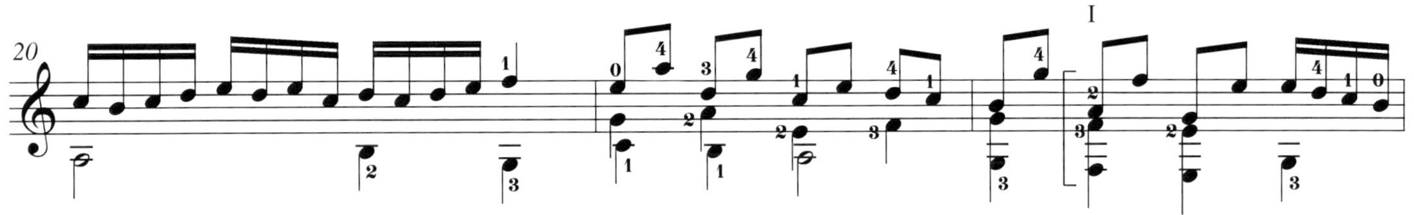

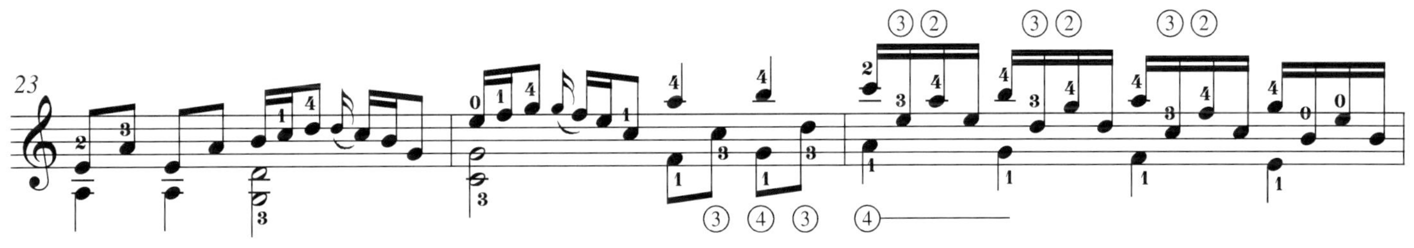

Mrs. Delany

Turlough O'Carolan

Allegretto

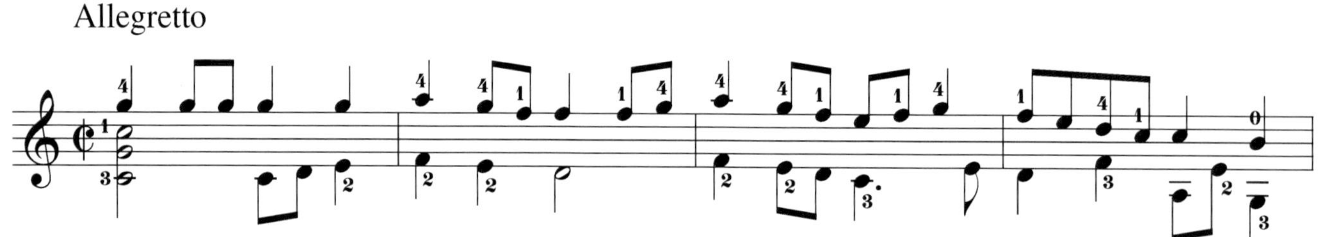

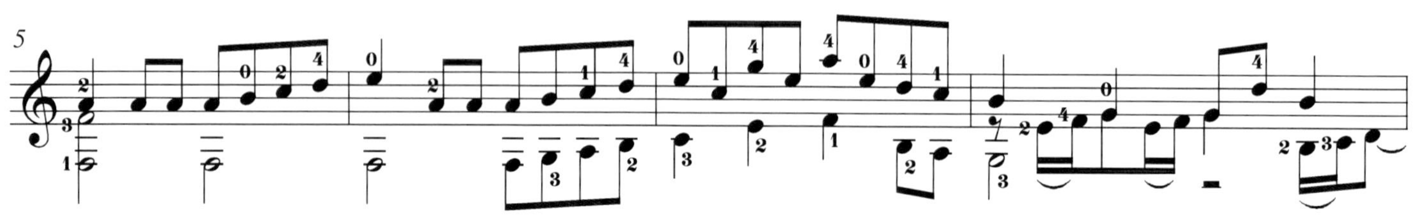

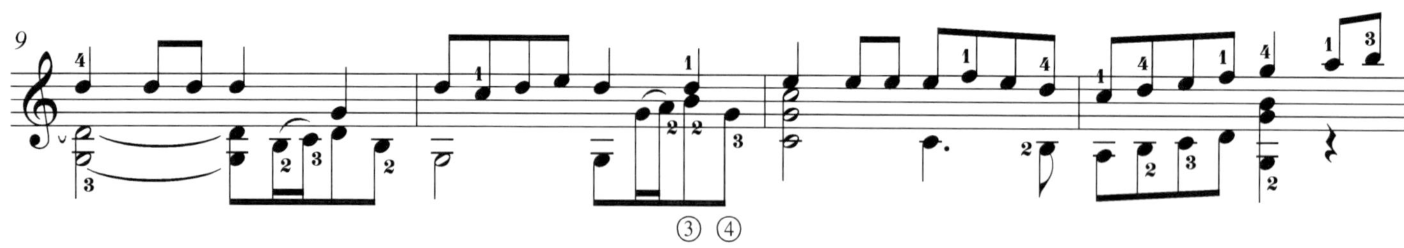

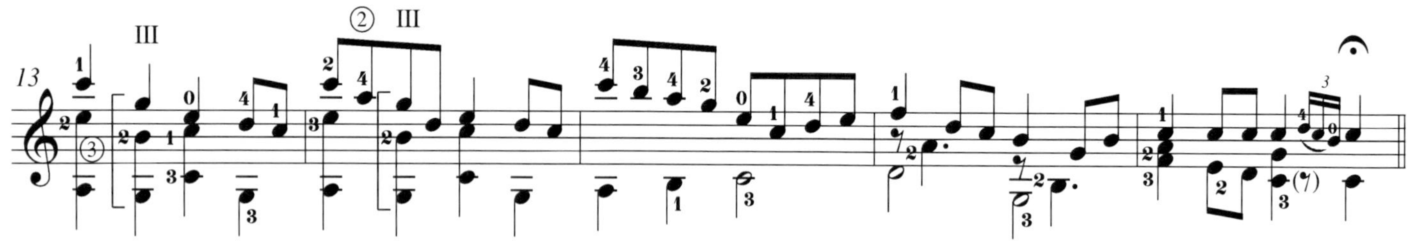

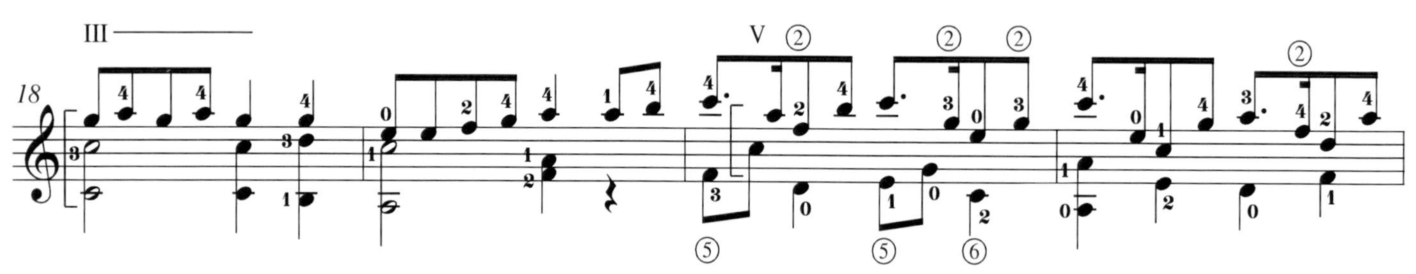

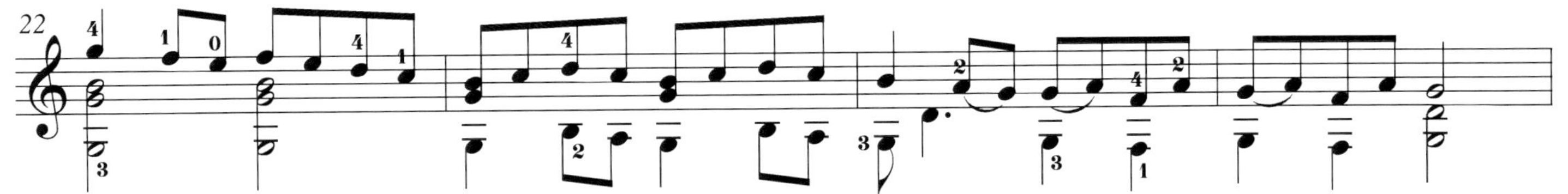

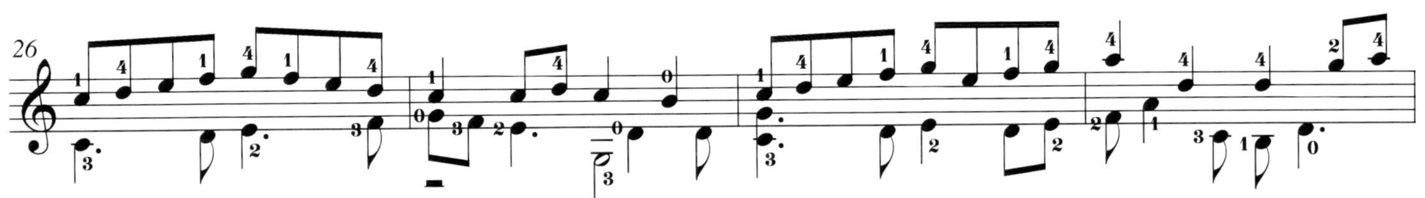

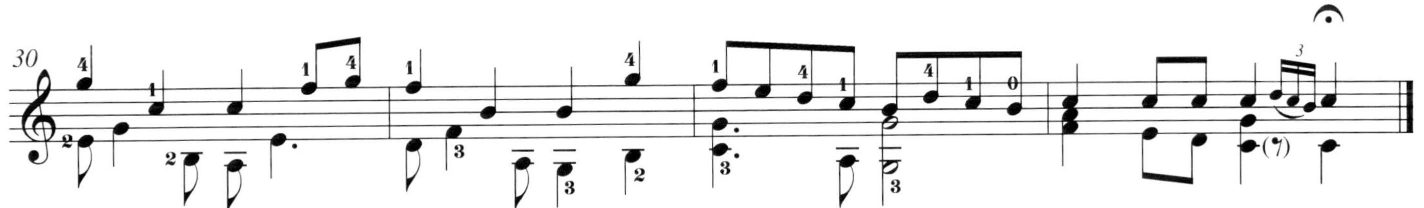

Sir Charles Coote

Turlough O'Carolan

Allegretto

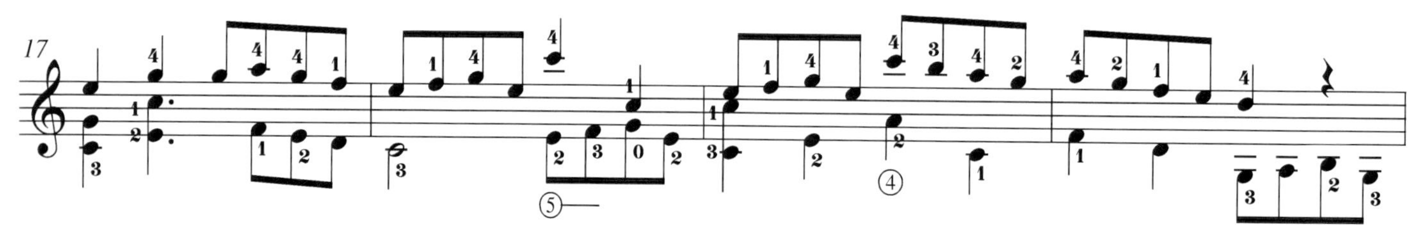

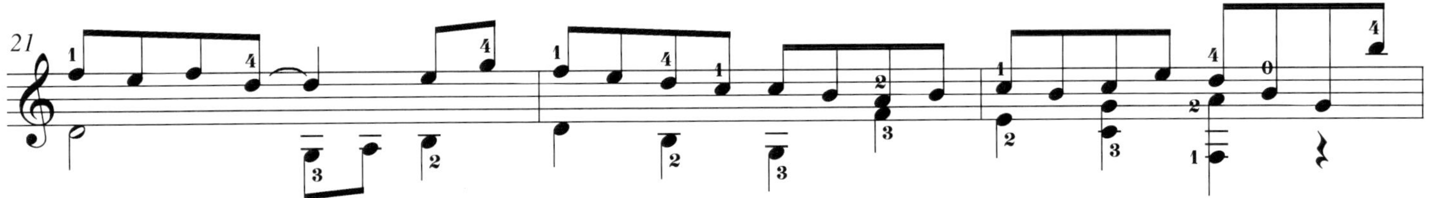
21

VIII
24

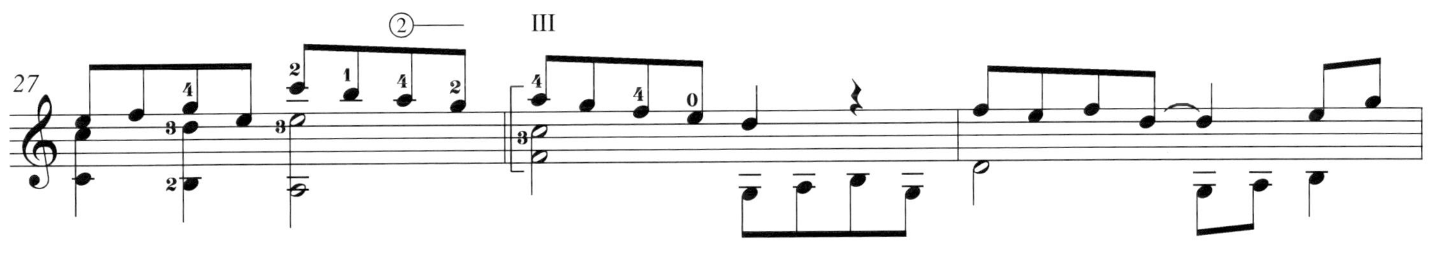
②
III
27

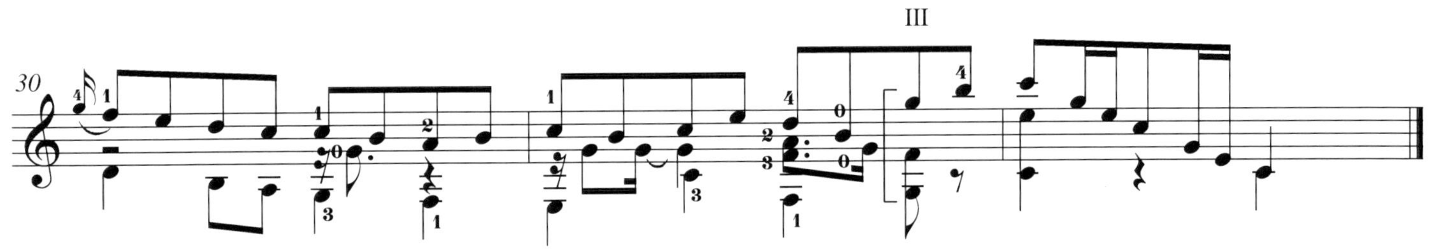
III
30

Daniel Kelly

Turlough O'Carolan

Moderato

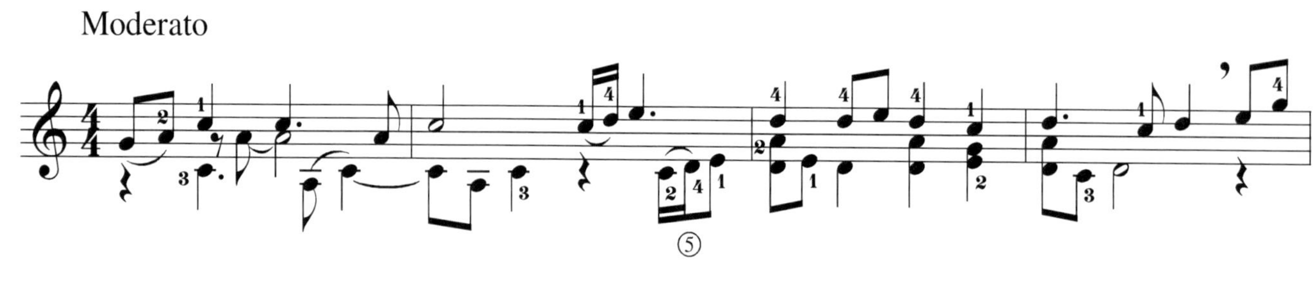

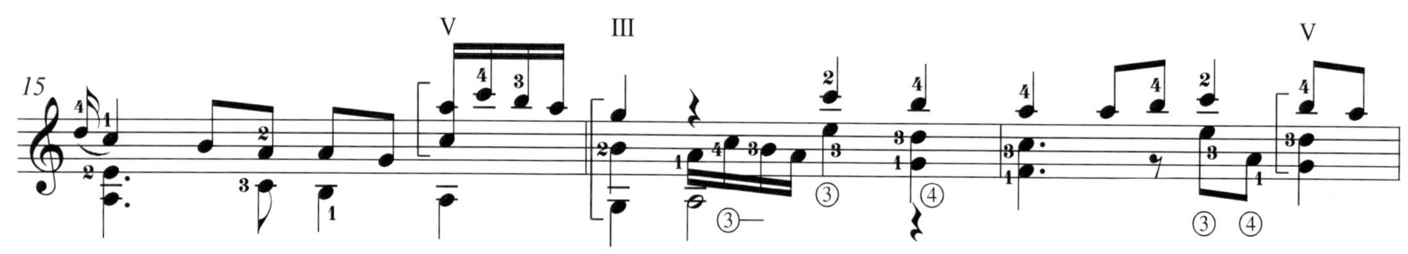

III
I
18

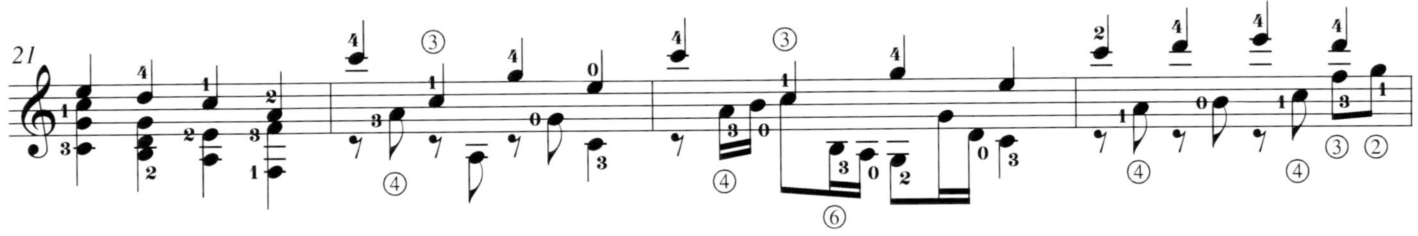
21

V
III
VIII
25

III
V
29

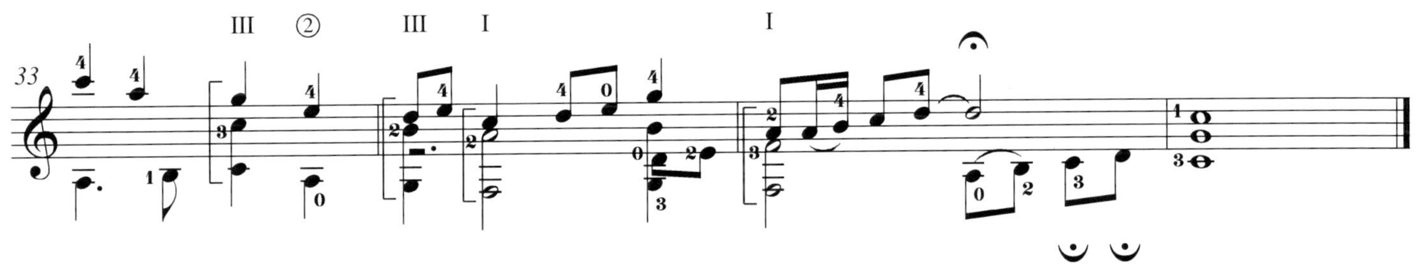
III
III
I
I
33

Catherine Martin

(Dorian Mode)

Turlough O'Carolan

Moderato

Catherine Martin

(Mixolydian Mode)

Turlough O'Carolan

Moderato

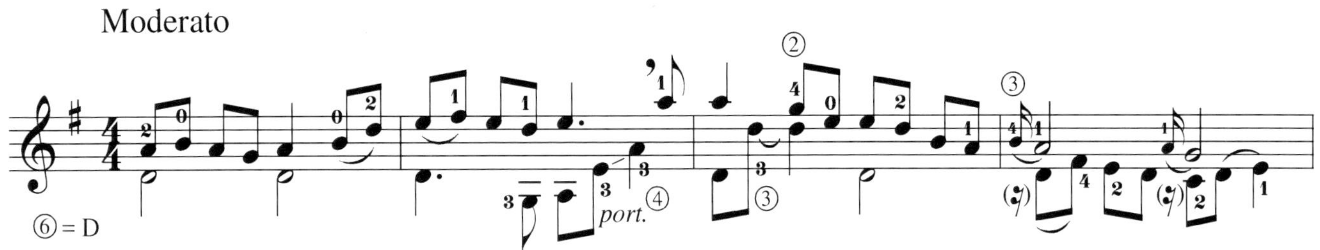

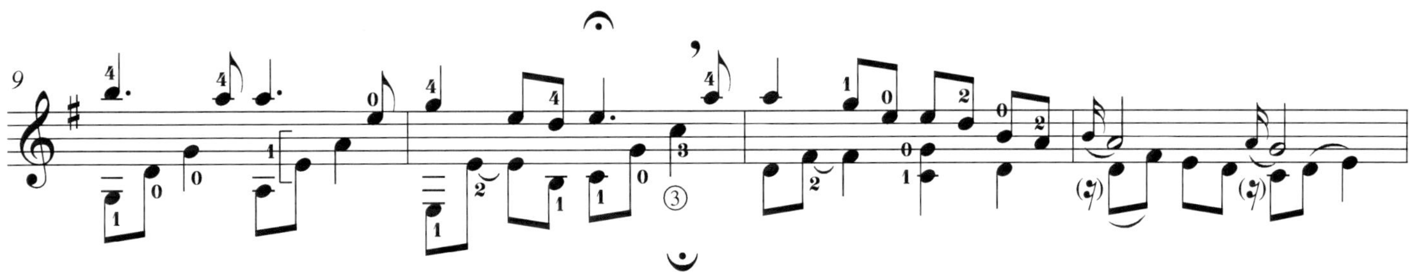

Brian Maguire

Turlough O'Carolan

Planxty O'Carolan
Originally Untitled

attributed to Turlough O'Carolan

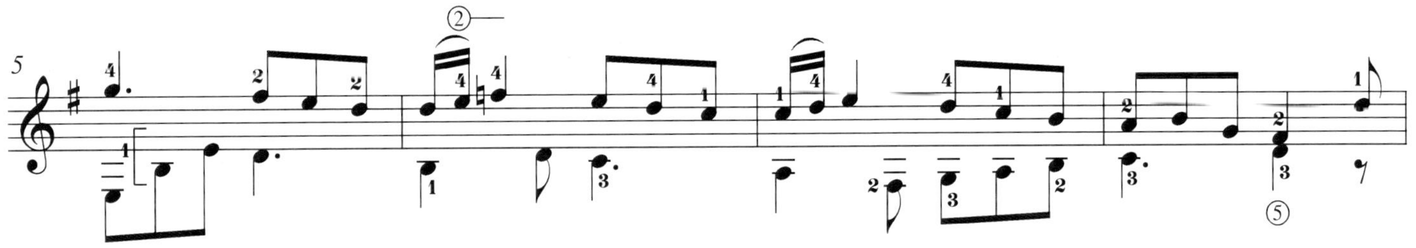

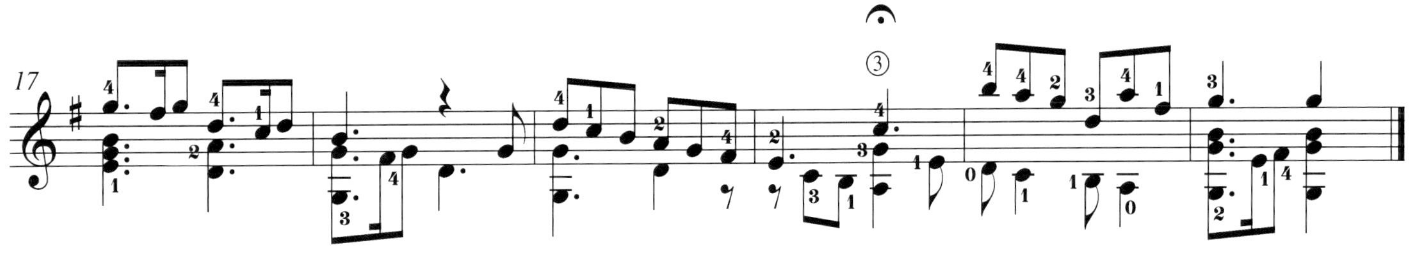

About the Author

Guido Böger

The guitarist Guido Böger was born and raised in Bad Lippspringe, North-Rhine Westphalia, Germany. He became interested in the classical guitar and its music in his youth, learning a variety of classical as well as popular literature. He was later admitted into the Cologne College of Music, where he majored in classical guitar. Through later studies, he then completed the "Reifeprüfung" (the German Master of Music Degree in Performance) at the Music College of Aachen, Germany. Alongside his teaching commitments at area Schools of Music, also at the University of Paderborn, Germany, he performs in numerous concerts both as a soloist, and in a variety of chamber music capacities. In 1993, Guido Böger was featured on the CD "Hexachord–New Music for Two Guitars". Since 1994, he has also performed regularly together with his wife, the soprano Meg Fitzgerald, as the Duo "Chitarra Canta", presenting a variety of Art Song, Celtic and jazz-classics programs. In 2001 they recorded the CD "Aisling - Irish Art Songs & Music". Through the demands of this concert work, he began writing more arrangements for voice and guitar, as well as solo settings of various music styles for the guitar. In recent years, he has released a collection of his arrangements of German Lieder for voice and guitar, "Und Wüssten's die Blumen..." from works by Fanny (Mendelssohn) Hensel, with Furore Editions of Kassel, Germany, as well as having worked with the modern German composer Günther Becker in editing his "Vier Studien" (Four Etudes) for solo guitar, with Edition Gravis, in Brühl, Germany. Guido Böger started working with Mel Bay Publications, Inc. in 2002 and, since the release of the first volume in 2010, he continues to arrange the complete works of Turlough O'Carolan for classical guitar.